What others are saying about this book . . .

We appreciate Peter Lumpkins' contribution to this crucial issue. We applaud all genuine efforts to convince followers of Jesus that the use of alcoholic beverages in any form is inconsistent with the lifestyle of an obedient Christian in the 21st century.

Richard Land, president
Ethics and Religious Liberty Commission, Southern Baptist Convention

A postmodern era of indulgence brands advocacy of abstinence from beverage alcohol as legalism worthy of the Pharisees, even as it gurgles its way to an ever-increasing embrace of the world. But Peter Lumpkins in *Alcohol Today: Abstinence in an Age of Indulgence* demonstrates why abstinence not only is wisdom but also a matter of obedience to Christ and holiness before God.

Paige Patterson, president
Southwestern Baptist Theological Seminary
Fort Worth, TX

Peter Lumpkins has done an amazing piece of work. He has explored the various views on the question of drinking "recreational alcohol" (booze) by disciples of Jesus. With the precision of a surgeon he dissects the views and then stitches them together for an overall answer to the question. This is the first book of this nature that I have read in years—the best argument in print against the outlandish and inaccurate views of "not use but abuse." Every preacher should make this a must-read.

John Sullivan, executive director-treasurer
Florida Baptist Convention

Peter Lumpkins' book calls us back to biblical convictions. Peter "rightly divides the word of truth", glorifies the Lord Jesus Christ, and provides a firm foundation for 21st-century believers in a Laodicean age.

Roger Freeman, senior pastor
First Baptist Church, Clarksville, TN
Past president, Tennessee Baptist Convention

Peter Lumpkins provides an exhaustive, in-depth investigation into the use of alcohol as a beverage. He reaches the conclusion that this usage is unwise, unhelpful, and unscriptural. I applaud him for his work and commend this read to all interested in thoroughly considering this issue.

Jim Richards, executive director
Southern Baptists of Texas Convention
Past first vice-president, Southern Baptist Convention

Our culture says "no harm, no foul". But as Peter Lumpkins points out in *Alcohol Today*, our responsibility is not defined only by the boundaries of the legal system. We must also surrender to biblical teaching and moral law. While being tolerant is not in vogue, doing so is not always biblical. Our tolerance must be in love—showing tolerance to those who do not know Christ—not in the issues that damage biblical integrity.

R. Chris Reynolds, senior pastor and president
Mount Zion Baptist Church and Christian Academy, Jonesboro, GA

At a time when purity within the evangelical church is being sacrificed at the altar of unity and holiness is asked to bow to pragmatism, Peter Lumpkins delivers a clarion call for the church to behave as the pure bride of Christ with respect to the consumption of alcohol. With biblical exegesis, philosophical effectiveness, and journalistic excellence Peter reveals the biblical case for abstinence for a generation which seems to be searching for biblical truth. Peter has demonstrated boldness, scholarship and genuineness on an issue that has far-reaching effects both within and without the walls of the church.

Bradley D. Reynolds, assistant professor of Christian education
Southeastern Baptist Theological Seminary

Peter Lumpkins' new book is a great vehicle that will help pastors, church leaders, and Christian families rediscover the biblical basis and common-sense reasons for promoting abstinence. If pastors and churches again will boldly teach the value of abstinence, elected officials may be motivated to stop legislating alcohol expansion. Peter's book could become the catalyst our nation needs to stop the gradual acceptance of moderation and return the churches of America and, hopefully our culture, to the biblical teaching of abstinence.

Joe Godfrey, executive director
Alabama Citizens Action Program

Four decades ago when I responded to God's call to the gospel ministry, the thought that theologically conservative Baptist leaders would discuss the wisdom of alcohol consumption among Christians much less pastors never would have entered my mind. But this very debate is bubbling to the surface now in our day when the the culture around us more and more invades the church instead of the church being the salt and light we are called to be. This volume will be a valued resource to those who hold to abstinence, a way to engage the debate for those who do not, and a vital encouragement to young Christians who are seeking to make their own way through this debate. Read it and reap.

O.S. Hawkins, president
GuideStone Financial Resources

ALCOHOL TODAY:

ABSTINENCE IN AN AGE OF INDULGENCE

PETER LUMPKINS

FOREWORD BY DR. JERRY VINES

HANNIBAL BOOKS
www.hannibalbooks.com

Printed in the United States of America
by Lightning Source, Inc.
Cover design by Dennis Davidson
Unless otherwise indicated,
all Scripture taken from the King James Version
of the Holy Bible. Used by permission.
Library of Congress Control Number: 2009927306
ISBN 978-1-934749-52-4

Hannibal Books
P.O. Box 461592
Garland, Texas 75046
1-800-747-0738
www.hannibalbooks.com

Dedication

to my wife, Kathy Lynn, who's been the love of my life for 36 years and with whose encouragement, patience, and undying support this book now exists.

Acknowledgements

Wise King Solomon said best, *To every thing there is a season, and a time to every purpose under the heaven* (Eccl. 3:1). A time for this book to be written and published finally has arrived. The time is now. When I resigned my last church in which I was fortunate to serve as pastor, this book is the fulfillment of the vision God gave me then. Deep within I knew God was giving me a commission in a new direction for ministry—a ministry of writing. I hope, by the grace of God, I die with pen in hand. For the rest of my days I want to communicate Him through the written word.

So many people contributed in some way to this work. First, I thank my wife for her patience in putting up with me while I was so focused on this work, not to mention her continual encouragement to finish such a needed book. Also, I thank Judy Louderback for her assistance in putting the manuscript together. Judy served as my administrative assistant for five years during my last assignment as pastor. No one could ask for a better assistant.

Pastor David Brumbelow has been nonstop in his encouragement, his support, and his enthusiasm for this book. David made valuable suggestions to the manuscript—suggestions I took and believe the book is better for it. Also, Dr. Malcolm Yarnell suffered through large portions of the manuscript. He offered priceless ways to make my point stronger and more consistent with biblical truth. Thank you.

My deep appreciation for Dr. Jerry Vines and his ministry cannot be overstated. He remains both a statesman and prophet among Southern Baptists, as well as a premier expositor of the Word of God. His foreword to this volume is gold. In addition, I cannot miss stating my gratitude to Hannibal Books in its decision to publish this work. Especially, I thank Louis and Kay Moore, who must be the most encouraging folk imaginable with whom to publish a book.

Yet, even with all the help I've received, when all is said, the responsibility for any errors rests with me. I only trust this book will assist someone to make moral, biblical decisions about consuming intoxicating beverages.

May our Lord Jesus Christ be pleased to use this book for His Glory.

With that, I am . . .

Peter Lumpkins
Spring 2009

Contents

Foreword

In the 50-plus years of my ministry as a gospel preacher and Southern Baptist pastor I have witnessed a definite shift relating to the alcohol issue. In the earlier years virtually every church and pastor of all denominations united against the use and sale of alcoholic beverages.

Then some churches and pastors fell silent. Today we see many churches in which the use of alcohol is commonly accepted. Even more disturbing, some pastors speak in favor of moderation in the use of intoxicating beverages. Some themselves drink. This greatly concerns me. It can portend only heartache and tragedy ahead.

The common mantra we hear is, "The Bible condemns the abuse of alcohol, not the use of alcohol". This is widely assumed to be correct. D.A. Carson, in his *Exegetical Fallacies*, mentions a logical fallacy he calls "cavalier dismissal"—that is, to routinely dismiss, ignore, or even lampoon a viewpoint and not give it a fair hearing. This is done today about the view that the Bible condemns the use of intoxicating beverages.

Dr. Peter Lumpkins has dropped a bombshell in the current climate of laxity relative to Christians and alcohol. This excellent book is a thorough, thoughtful, scholarly presentation of the arguments for total abstinence. Good scholarship relative to the total abstinence position is available, but much of it is from older writers. This current work will be a valuable resource for pastors and churches wanting to lift high the standards of holiness and right conduct among their members.

Dr. Lumpkins has arranged the chapters of his book into three helpful sections. Part 1 gives his reasons for writing the book, the tragic compromises too many churches have made about alcohol, and an exposé of the lie that Prohibition didn't work.

Part 2 is a very helpful examination of the various options available when the consumption of intoxicating substances is concerned. In my opinion his observation that arguments about moderation in the use of alcohol also can be applied to cocaine and other addictive substances is irrefutable.

Part 3 is the most important section. He gives a very complete and convincing exposition of the Bible passages relating to wine, the Old Testament Book of Proverbs' texts relating to wine, and the much-abused passage in John 2 in which Jesus turns the water into wine. The faithful exegete of Scripture who believes in the inerrancy of Scripture is faced with a dilemma. Many passages clearly commend the use of wine. An equal number of passages clearly condemn the use of alcohol. For an inerrantist, the question becomes—how can God condemn on the one hand what He commends on the other? Dr. Lumpkins solves the dilemma for the Bible-believing exegete. I encourage you not to "cavalierly dismiss" Dr. Lumpkins' work that shows a solution to this dilemma.

I pray this book will become a standard in the field of total abstinence about intoxicating beverages. The lives of thousands of pastors, their families, and the families of their congregations are at stake. Too many already have started down the slippery slope of moderation. My prayer is that this helpful volume will be a rope to pull many to safety.

Jerry Vines
President, Jerry Vines Ministries, Inc.
Pastor emeritus, First Baptist Church, Jacksonville, FL
Twice-elected president of the Southern Baptist Convention

Part 1

Chapter 1

Why This Book

While I sat in the coffee shop finalizing my outline for this project, my eyes drifted from the page I was writing to the screen of my laptop before me. My eyes latched onto the headline, "College President Resigns over Alcohol Incident." Thinking it was just another typical story, I clicked the link; a picture loaded. In the lake sat a boat with several college students and one older man in his 50s. I quickly learned that the older man was the college president.

A closer look summoned from my inner spirit a scalding-hot flush of anger. Why such raw emotion? Firmly gripped in the president's hands, a keg of beer dangled over the mouth of a young female student. Her jaws appeared swollen with the foamy substance culture christens the "fifth element" after water, fire, earth, and wind. Those of us not so captivated by its mythical powers just call it *beer*.

The young woman's physique, hairstyle, and age immediately sketched in my mind pencil drawings of my beautiful daughters. I imagine them recklessly under the influence of a hypocritical authority figure sworn to protect their best interests. Instead he breaches my trust and pillages their consciences with a pathetically amoral approach to an incredibly powerful addictive drug—*beverage alcohol*. As I look deeper into the picture, I can almost see the president's lips moving as I hear him mumble to my precious little girl, "Eat, drink, and be merry; for tomorrow we die."

Frankly, to this day the hot flush still smolders. The image of an irresponsible educator pouring a dangerous drug into the mouth of some daddy's little girl indelibly pierces my inner soul. It tattooes righteous anger in all its glaring colors. I feel fully David's hot but holy rage as he stares with shock at Israel's taunting enemy and blurts out: *Who is this uncircumcised Philistine, that he should defy the armies of the living God?* (1 Sam. 17:26). The fact that I am not within the ancient sling's distance was best for me and the college president.

The story continues. The college trustees quickly gather to assess the damage. After considering the president's defense that he neither broke school policy nor criminal law—never mind the breached trust, which remains a moral crime all its own to both student and parents—the trustees punish the president by endowing him with almost a half-million dollar settlement. They mention nothing about whether the president acted irresponsibly by encouraging the consumption of underage drinking nor his breach of public trust. Nothing.

Once again I realize a book like this one needs desperately to exist.

The 2007 Youth Risk Behavior Survey found that among high-school students, when asked whether, during the past 30 days, alcohol had been consumed, 45 percent drank some amount of alcohol. Also, an estimated 46 million persons ages 12 or older are "binge drinkers" (ASA, 2009). According to the Centers for Disease Control and Prevention *binge drinking* is defined for scientific purposes as "drinking five or more drinks on the same occasion (i.e., at the same time or within a couple of hours of each other) on at least one day in the past 30 days" (CDC, 2009). More than one-fifth (23.3 percent) of persons aged 12 or older participated in binge drinking at least once in the 30 days before the survey in 2007. This translates to about 57.8 million people.

Even more disheartening is the fact that although the numbers decrease with age, a shocking number of heavy drinkers begin at the tender age of 12. In 2006—the latest available statistics—117,000 "binge drinkers" between the ages of 12 and

13 were boozing it up. Imagine: on average in excess of 300 drinking "binges" per day by 12- to 13-year olds alone. Overall, underage drinkers consumed about 11 percent of all the alcohol purchased in the United States in 2002, with the overwhelming majority of alcohol consumed in a risky fashion. In addition approximately 90 percent of alcohol consumed by youth under the age of 21 years is in "risky" drinking (i.e., binge drinking).

Compare such sad numbers of our young people who are already trapped in a world of irresponsible drink to the horrifying image of a publicly entrusted college administrator pouring from a keg into the mouth of one of these unfortunate youth an addictive potion such as beverage alcohol. If such imagined snapshots do nothing to you as a parent, a grandparent, a pastor, a student pastor, a politician, or just a concerned citizen, then as a civilized society we very well may be beyond hope. Such a scenario is a major trajectory for this book—a simple but profound concern for our next generation.

My wife and I have been divinely blessed with three children who now are grown and married. Last year we just had our first grandbaby and will have two more additions before this book goes to print! What a thrill to see our beautiful little Sofia as she begins to walk, talk, and gain footing in this world our Lord preserves for her. Yet even the fleeting thought of her trapped in the jaws of the liquor industry frightens me. Liquor manufacturers cater to youthful tastes by designing new alcohol products that significantly add to the underage drinking problem. Sweet, fruity beverages deceptively appearing like innocuous soft drinks, malt liquors, "alcopops," etc. possess levels of alcohol content comparable to standard beers but are available at low prices.

Marketing ploys with gimmicks such as containers that resemble "TNT explosives" or alcoholic beverages with neon colors that change the color of the drinker's tongue are geared specifically with youthful drinkers in mind. Of course for the most part any question raised concerning the impact these marketing ploys have in tempting the underaged to imbibe is met with an angelic-like denial.

Apparently the wine industry now has caught the profit-driven vision of recruiting our young and no longer sits idly by as beer brings in the bucks from the latest gimmick to entice young recruits. Said one winery at a stunning but candid moment: " . . . it is imperative to attract new generations who will be the wine drinkers of the future. Young adults feel lost in the world of wine . . ." (ACB, 2009). Designer wines marketed specifically to music tastes (such as rap, hip-hop, country, new age, etc.) of our young, their hope is, will fix the budget crunch the industry experiences.

Connecting this youthfully designed marketeering with the culture of extreme so vividly illustrated by binge drinking—promoted even by college administrators, who are entrusted publicly with our children's welfare—and the result becomes frightening. Can we not see the horrid end to our naïve flirtation with societal extinction by peddling our sons and daughters to the pleasure-producers of this age? My answer to this question is partly why this book exists.

Concern for today's young people, if nothing else, catapults us to consider this profound problem which, unfortunately, is not an issue specifically of the young. In fact it is a disease we've passed on to them. *Indulging adults of this age infect their own offspring with the culture of extreme and excess.* We want . . . and want more . . . then want some more. Even though we get and got, we live for more get. Our appetites appear never fulfilled, our thirsts never quenched. Thus we pursue. We seek. We want. We desire. Always desire. Pleasure is no human *privilege*; pleasure is a human *right*.

Perhaps such excess is implicit to our incurable addiction to freedom. Not that freedom is not a good thing; to the contrary, freedom not only is intrinsic to the American spirit, freedom also is built into the structure of our being made in God's image. Freedom can lose its way, however, and travel down a dangerous road. This can lead to a kind of warped demand that insists against any and all who attempt to restrain, "I have a right," "I am free," "Who are you to tell me I can't?"

Again this skewed sense of freedom easily surfaces concerning making available alcoholic substances. Just the mention of restricting access to alcoholic beverages draws the ire of the masses. Immediately one is charged with promoting the old, failed "Prohibition"—the universal talking point of every advocate of alcoholic beverage. Nor is this just the culture at large that hurls the charge of restricting rights. Sadly the religious public may blow the loudest horn!

The church's conviction vanishing

The Christian church (especially the Protestant side) that was virtually unanimous in support of the "old, failed Prohibition" policies will go on record quickly these days, if asked, that imbibing alcoholic beverages is not as bad as it used to be. Even though a century ago the church was certain imbibing was a carnal evil, it remains certain no longer. Curiously church representatives never get around to explaining why imbibing alcohol was carnality then but not carnality now. Instead assumptions of the social acceptability of drinking are normalized, while they continue to sing the same melody about not legislating morality. Strange. The reality is, one is stringently pressed to name any one thing that can be legislated that is *not* morality—*someone's morality*.

What can one expect even from some of the most conservative Christian communions when suggesting the recreational use of addictive drugs such as alcohol is neither moral nor biblical? Well, when I make this suggestion, my body hopelessly reels from rapid-fire rocks the defenders of **moderate** drink cast. By far the rock so often tossed includes a personally hand-painted note on its surface—"pharisaical legalism." If someone suspects the position that one publicly advocates is abstaining from intoxicating beverages, one might as well go ahead and duck while time remains. How easily some Christians mistake Jesus' words *upon this rock I will build my church* (Mt. 16:18) for "from this church I'll cast my rocks"!

One professor from a Southern Baptist seminary had this to say: "Are alcoholic beverages a good thing? Sure! Within moderate amounts, of course. In fact, don't ever let anybody tell you any differently. If they do, they are closet Roman Catholics who are imposing pharisaical legalism on you. They do not hold to Scripture. They sacrifice biblical integrity" (more on this shortly).

One recalls the words Bishop F. W. Farrar spoke more than a century ago as he lamented both media and churchpeople who ambushed total abstinence from alcoholic beverages: "The secular press tells us that the advocates of total abstinence are impracticable fanatics and wrong-headed Pharisees; the religious press tells us that abstinence is a much poorer stage of virtue than moderation, and that, by declining wine and beer, we fall far below the attainment of those moral athletes who, to their hearts' content, indulge themselves in both" (Farrar, 1879).

Similar to the enemies of abstinence with whom Farrar contended, this professor's idea of the abstinence standard evidently reduces to moral legalism, denial of Scripture, and absence of integrity. I'd say those are three hefty rocks. If you mention *abstinence*, be ready to duck!

Thus, the idea that the least talk of moral restraint destroys freedom is not a position embedded in the culture of extreme and excess alone; the idea is deeply embedded in church subculture as well. This remains another reason this book begs for existence: *The church has, in major proportions, conceded its historic role as the moral conscience of our culture, particularly as it forfeited its once-strong position on abstinence from intoxicating beverages for pleasurable purposes.*

The church—especially what's known as the evangelical church, the piece of pie to which I belong—increasingly speaks a message of moderation about intoxicating beverages. One rightly may ask, "What substantial help does the message of moderation offer to our next generation?" In fact the message the church proclaims about moderately consuming alcohol is, in the end, really no different from the more responsible messages from the culture at large. The new song the evangelical choir sings is short, pithy and to the point: *The Bible does not condemn the use of alcohol; the Bible condemns the abuse of alcohol.* What difference is that, in effect, from saying "Drink but don't drive" or "Drink but be careful how much"? Tragically the church that abandons abstinence partners itself with the more morally astute politic of secular culture. It moves in lockstep with the culture of extreme and excess and forsakes the biblically-driven ethic of abstinence. It pens a message morally legible to our young generation: "Drinking is perfectly OK. Consuming intoxicating beverages for pleasure is an acceptable and moral social custom. Do it. But be particularly careful to neither abuse nor drink irresponsibly."

Of course this is not literally written to the young generation. After all such things as laws exist against underage drinking. Nonetheless those millions of underage drinkers somehow found themselves access to the intoxicant. Recall what we mentioned earlier. Not only did underage drinkers consume 11 percent of all alcoholic beverages purchased in the United States in 2002, but also the vast majority of the alcohol purchased for underage consumption was consumed in binge and heavy drinking. Thus our children are getting the booze. The message about booze seems all too obvious: "Drinking is cool. Even the church says drinking is cool, if we're careful about the amount." The sad reality is, the church without the abstinence standard—consciously or unconsciously—plays a co-conspirator part in promoting such a message. If Christian parents, pastors, student ministers, and Bible-believing churches remain unmoved by such, one must consider whether or not we have a culture worth salvaging.

Consider with me something else. Mix the relaxed feeling young people inevitably experience when they hear over and over again that even the church supports drinking—at least in moderate amounts—with the natural temperament of the young. What do you think will result? When that batch of cookies pops out of the oven, do not be surprised if they are burnt black. Do we honestly think teen-agers possess the developed psychological equipment to practice moderation in anything, much less highly addictive intoxicants? Once again studies show that young people who drink are far more likely to drink more heavily than do adults. Also the overwhelming majority of binge drinkers are young drinkers. Moderation? Not on your life.

Like it or not the church that preaches and practices moderation toward intoxicating beverages for pleasurable purposes cannot escape partial blame for giving to our next generation an uncertain sound on moral restraint. That stands as yet another reason why this book must have a heartbeat. In the next chapter I intend to take this idea one step further.

My story

Finally I'd better "fess up" and share a bit of my own personal story. This too stands as a fitting motivation for writing this book. I grew up in middle Tennessee, the last of 12 children reared in a little four-room house. Our home sat at the bottom of Coon Creek Hollow only a rock's throw from a heavily used railway.

Beside our little house ran Coon Creek. Then, the stream seemed colossal. It had a thundering waterfall less than 10 yards from the front porch. During the summers my siblings and I swam for hours in what we called "the big hole". Our swimming hole also doubled for the bathtub as weather allowed (that's right, we had no plumbing in our house).

As I've visited the old homeplace since, however, the "colossal" stream is only about six-feet wide. The "big hole" isn't more than three-feet deep at most. Oh, and the "thundering waterfall" is 12 inches more or less.

Because Coon Creek ran through the hollow, the railroad built a trestle over it. In fact our outhouse sat almost under the trestle. Believe me: things could get interesting when schedules overlapped between our occupying the outhouse and the railroad's daily use of the trestle! I spent the first 17 years of my life juggling those apples.

My family was large but extremely poor. Though we were not a "Christian home", a measure of respect for God was both assumed and instilled. I will forever be grateful that my parents faithfully arranged for transportation to Sunday school and church. In my childhood I had my first encounter with God. And, though I was not converted to Jesus Christ until I was adult, the early formative years I experienced through faithful biblical teaching branded spiritual marks on my soul about the Christian faith. I never forgot.

Unfortunately my childhood also was the time in which I had my first encounter with alcohol. I don't remember the age when I tasted beer for the first time, but I definitely was young. In fact truthfully I cannot recall a period in which I was not drinking. Oh, I didn't drink a lot as a young boy. But then again a young boy can get drunk on very little.

My daddy was virtually uneducated, yet he managed to rear 12 children on his humble earnings from a chemical plant in a neighboring city. Three images remain with me about Daddy. Daddy loved fishing. Whenever he could, he was setting the minnow baskets in the little creek that ran by our house. He hoped to catch the desirable *chub minners* as he called them. For him "chubs" offered the most promise to land a small-mouth bass from Sugar Creek.

Another image that appears whenever I think of my dad is baseball. He sat glued to the black-and-white every Saturday when the Braves played. Next to fishing, baseball was Daddy's primary pastime. Indeed baseball was the last conscious activity Daddy experienced in this life. While watching the 1970 World Series, his lungs began to fill. When the game ended, Mama took him to the hospital. He died about an hour later. I was 16.

The third image is an uncomely one. Daddy loved beer— lots of beer. The truth be told, I can barely recall images of my daddy without also recalling the beer in his hand. Daddy's beer is what I drank when I was a child. This began only as a sip from his can when I would fetch him one from the fridge. It would graduate to swiping whole cans of beer and heading for the nearby woods.

I was barely 16-years old when my daddy died. From his death until I married, rarely a week went by I did not drink until I passed out. I share this snapshot of my life not to sensationalize my life. I do so instead because I want the reader to realize my personal identification with this issue. By experience I know the destruction intoxicating beverages bring. The social, leisurely perspective many embrace when dealing with this issue remains no luxury for me, nor does it to countless others who've seen and experienced this destructive phenomenon up close. Alcohol's acid kills whatever or whomever it touches.

Admittedly some may see my personal circumstances as tainting the case I make for abstinence. Perhaps my reasoning, they argue, may be emotionally driven. Consequently the moral reasoning I offer for abstinence becomes suspect because of my bias against alcohol. To those who may similarly rationalize, I say but two things in response.

First, I'm not sure my bias about this issue should concern us. My candid telling you of my tragic story should bleed the air out of that balloon. Also, one could ask, "Who exists as a biased-free being?" If being biased-free is the criteria for valid contribution, few, if any, could ever validly qualify. Being biased is not what makes a person's view suspect. Rather, being bias-blind is the culprit tragically tainting a person's perspective. I'm fully aware of the up-close connection I have with this issue.

The second thing I say in response is this: I concede the charge may be true. My objection aside, perhaps I really am so emotionally involved in this issue that my moral reasoning is hopelessly clouded and thus consequently offers little contribution to the needed discussion on the recreational use of intoxicants. Nor can I or will I deny the sympathy I possess for the millions of young people caught in the jaws of the death trap known as alcohol. So be it. My sole recourse, then, is to leave such judgment in the hands of the reading public. I only ask my readers to consider the argument I propose in the following pages with the same unbiased perspective expected of me.

Chapter 2

The Church Changing Its Mind on Drink

In January 2007 I began a series of online essays on *Wine, the Bible, and the Believer.* For a period of approximately a month and a half, I published 19 short essays dealing specifically with this issue. I did this mostly because I desired to inject another view that not only dissents from many of the high-profile Baptist blogs (many are vocally moderationist) but also represents what I believe to be the majority view of grassroots Southern Baptists.

My eyes opened

In early 2008 a seminary professor's short essay caught my attention. I had often read the professor's site; thus issues we disagreed about were present. The disagreements, however, were mostly insignificant—nothing substantial. Something about one posted essay was different, however; the least bit of vagueness was not present in the words he wrote. The professor's words oozed clarity and definiteness. No one missed his meaning:

Every time someone argues that alcohol consumption is unbiblical, they have rejected the sufficiency of Scripture and become a closet Roman Catholic . . ..

Every time someone imposes their private practices concerning alcohol on others, they have become a closet Pharisee . . ..

I can think of zero good reasons to replace Scripture with tradition . . . making alcohol consumption a practice that disqualifies someone from denominational service.

Southern Baptists who drink alcohol . . . [should recognize] . . . that the convention is filled with weaker brothers who don't yet get it.

. . . the integrity of Scripture . . . is at stake.

Now to be perfectly fair to the professor, he humbly conceded with a gracious spirit on the comment thread indicating his descriptive language concerning **abstentionists** such as myself and millions of other Southern Baptists was not what one would call winsome. And we thank him for such and hope under our Lord all of us may speak—even if we necessarily must speak tough—with salt and light. Also, in only a matter of hours, the essay entitled "Unplugged on Alcohol" was literally "unplugged" from the Internet. Letters of apology were sent.

In further spirit of fairness, however, I must note that only recently another post had the same professor throwing a passing slap to abstentionists pertaining to alcohol. In pondering the question "Does the SBC Have a Future?" he wrote of the "tortured exegesis" of those who argue drinking alcohol is inherently sinful.

From the professor's words one gets the picture that abstentionists reject flat-out the sufficiency of Scripture. In addition his words give the impression that every time they open their mouths about abstention, they strangely morph into either a closet Roman Catholic or a Pharisee who allegedly cares nothing for Scripture but bases all on tradition. Just what the professor meant about "closet Roman Catholic" remains unclear. Presumably he meant to convey that those attempting to legalistically impose abstinence on others are by default acting as spiritual "popes" over everyone else. Whatever the case, this tar-baby tactic is used toward those who for more than a century and a half have held strong views against consuming alcoholic beverages.

And, just in case one who abstains from alcohol quotes the Bible, moderation advocates like the professor immediately tag it as "tortured exegesis" at work, since abstentionists obviously constitute the *weak believers* to which the Bible refers.

The most potent ridicule, however, is none of the above. By far the most hurtful rhetoric moderationists use toward those who abstain from alcohol and exhort abstinence is classifying them with unbelievers. No more blistery language does Jesus offer than to the Pharisees whom He righteously references as white-washed sepulchers, children of hell, and hypocritically moral buffoons (Mt. 23:1-39). Pharisees are just not nice people, nor are they considered believers. Why moderationists such as the professor lump abstentionists with them I do not understand. I do know it is unacceptable.

The irony inevitably is that not one micro-shred of Scripture was argued for or alluded to in the professor's exhortation for abstentionists to "cool it" on the alcohol issue. Rather, throughout the presentation, moderation and its trusty sidekick—*Scripture condemns the abuse of alcohol, not the use of alcohol*—galloped freely throughout the entire pasture. In the professor's presentation *moderation was everywhere the assumed biblical position.*

That brings us to the focus in this chapter: *the American church has slowly changed its mind on alcoholic consumption.* Given the fact that our culture all but pours its citizens their first glass of wine for free, what role does the church play in the drama of indulgent drinking that we are observing? And, can we be abstinent in an age of indulgence? The answer remains difficult to discern, I assure; nevertheless I am intent on trying. Indeed answers to these questions are what this book is all about.

The church then and now

With few exceptions virtually every Protestant denomination possesses a recorded history of its position on alcoholic beverages, whether that position be formal or informal. By *formal* is meant positions which, by virtue of the denominational structure (**ecclesiology**) of the faith community, are the official positions for the entire denomination. For example Presbyterians and Methodists have official positions on alcoholic beverages (among countless other issues). By *informal* is meant positions that are expressed in documents such as non-binding resolutions. The clearest example of expressing unofficial positions is the largest Protestant group in America, the Southern Baptist Convention. Since their inception in 1845 Southern Baptists have passed resolutions on virtually every significant social issue our country has faced (some would say insignificant as well!). And, while the resolutions cannot be considered formal—in the sense of official position on the issues—the resolutions should not be considered unpersuasive either.

What's fascinating in examining the denominational record of imbibing alcoholic beverages over the last century or so is the obvious change of heart the church at large has had. The Presbyterian Church was at the forefront of the **Temperance Movement** from the early 19th century until after **Prohibition** in the 1930s. Furthermore the Methodist Church offered more volunteers to the temperance cause than perhaps any other denomination. Now, however, Presbyterians along with Methodists boast stances on moderately imbibing alcohol. The recreational usage of intoxicating beverages is broadly acceptable.

The Assemblies of God history began a little later than that of many other evangelicals. However, this body's stance on alcoholic beverages has not wavered in more than a hundred years. Its official position states, "Alcoholic beverages should have no place in the life of the Christian. Let there be no doubt about where the Assemblies of God stand on this critical issue. We declare unequivocally that total abstinence from alcoholic beverages is the only acceptable way of life for the Christian" (Lee, 2009).

Dr. Edgar Lee, chair for the Commission on Doctrinal Purity for the General Council of the Assemblies of God, further indicated in correspondence with me, " . . .we are in process of reviewing and revising, as needed, all of our position papers, and the paper on alcohol consumption will almost certainly be revised like most of the others. It undoubtedly needs somewhat better exegetical underpinnings and some updating on the social devastation of alcoholism. But even when, and if, the paper is revised, I cannot imagine that our position on abstinence will be changed. Our leadership is strongly committed to abstinence and deeply concerned about the human toll of alcoholism."

Thus, the Assemblies of God record on abstinence remains unmoved and in clear contrast to many other Protestants, including both Presbyterians and Methodists who stood on the frontlines of the Temperance Movement in 19th-century America.

For more than a century and a half Southern Baptists have had no less consistency in their strong abstinence position. Even after Prohibition ended in 1933, the Southern Baptist Convention continued to publicly affirm abstinence.

In May 1886 the convention said: "RESOLVED, That we, as members of the Southern Baptist Convention, do most solemnly protest against its manufacture and sale, and pledge our influence in the exercise of our rights as citizens of this free country, socially, morally, religiously and in all other proper ways, to work for its speedy overthrow, and to this end we invoke the aid and blessing of Almighty God" (Resolution S., 1886).

A decade later as the Prohibition movement smoothly waxed on as it led the way in creating, in adherents' views, not only a more God-honoring culture but also a more stable democracy that could host best a robust pursuit of life, liberty, and happiness, again the Southern Baptist Convention agreed with the platform of social Prohibitionists. Not only so, but

Southern Baptists also verbalized their encouragement to discipline church members who insisted on consuming alcoholic substances for recreational purposes: "Furthermore, we announce it as the sense of this body that no person should be retained in the fellowship of a Baptist church who engages in the manufacture or sale of alcoholic liquors, either at wholesale or retail, who invests his money in the manufacture or sale of alcoholic liquors, or who rents his property to be used for distilleries, wholesale liquor houses, or saloons. Nor do we believe that any church should retain in its fellowship any member who drinks intoxicating liquors as a beverage, or visits saloons or drinking places for the purpose of such indulgence" (Resolution, 1896).

Is unity on abstinence among Southern Baptists over?

Beginning in 1886 up until 2006, no fewer than 40 resolutions pertaining to alcohol have been passed by Southern Baptists (Richard Land, 2008). All of these presumably presented the same message: *total abstinence from alcoholic beverages for pleasurable purposes.* In addition this consistent abstinence position remains fascinating not only because most other Protestant denominations have changed their positions away from total abstinence but also because Southern Baptists themselves disputed weighty issues over which they fought— and sometimes fought fiercely—but managed to remain publicly united on their view of intoxicating drink. Disputes over Baptist origins, evolution, modernism, neo-orthodoxy, biblical authorship, and biblical inspiration each had its turn to blossom on Baptist soil. Yet in their moral persuasion on partaking alcoholic beverages solely for pleasure, Southern Baptists remained firmly united—*total abstinence.*

While such a clear, consistent history Southern Baptists experienced in their stance against imbibing alcohol is to be commended, definite signs appear indicating the united stance they've professed is beginning to crack. The Southern Baptist

Convention that met in Greensboro, SC, in 2006 may be the most visible sign to date. What took place sent shockwaves through the convention.

Not having a public expression on record for 15 years, the resolutions committee proposed to the convention a resolution on alcohol. The fiery debate that followed this fed a media frenzy: *Southern Baptists appeared publicly divided on total abstinence*. The debate floor flooded with a stream of new but influential spokesmen for the ethics of moderation in drinking and not for abstinence. Though the resolution passed by a sizable majority, the debate appeared only to flame passion on both sides. It also served as an official notice to Southern Baptists—a notice indicating her historic unity on abstinence soon may become history itself.

One Florida pastor, known for leading the Calvinist Resurgence in the Southern Baptist Convention, spoke against the Greensboro resolution because the resolution struck him as "ill-conceived and unbiblical. We have enough problems dealing with real sins. We certainly don't need to *manufacture* more sins out of cultural preferences."

Of notable contrast 19th-century Southern Baptist scholar and seminary professor John Broadus did not hold as "manufacturing sin" the abstinence standard. Rather Broadus had another view: "I love the cause of Temperance . . . if there is any cause of earthly kind that is nearer and dearer to my heart than all beside, it is the cause of Temperance . . . That intemperance is an evil . . . it would be needless to demonstrate . . . The remedy for this evil is known to all. Experience has demonstrated that Total Abstinence, and Total Abstinence alone, can emancipate the slave from the bondage of Intemperance . . . let us never cease from our labors till the power of Intemperance shall have been trampled in the duel, and the proud flag of Total Abstinence shall wave upon every hill-top of our native land" (Broadus, 1845).

Nor does such controversy end at the convention. Southern

Baptist pastors publicly deny abstinence is biblical. An Oklahoma pastor who's been unusually vocal in other matters makes history by being the first contemporary Southern Baptist to actually publish in a book views sympathetic to drinking alcohol in moderation while judging those who insist on biblically-based abstinence to be sinning against God.

I doubt Oklahoma Southern Baptists fully knew their past two-term president of the Baptist General Convention of Oklahoma held such libertine views of alcohol when they elected him. However, his views no longer lack doubt: "The idea that to drink a glass of wine, or any other alcoholic beverage, is a sin against God is so foreign to the teaching of the inspired, inerrant Word of God that for anyone to say to a Christian who has no abstinence conviction, 'You are sinning against God when you drink a glass of wine' is a sin in itself" (Burleson, 2009). On his highly frequented blog the author made further remarks about witnessing to a lost person over a glass of wine, a drink concerning which he himself initiated.

Up until now global culture's laxity toward elegant and fortified wines stood as the preferred query to loosen our abstinence resolve. "What are our missionaries supposed to do when they're served wine in acceptable atmospheres—offend those they're attempting to reach with the Gospel?" This question remains a well-worn dilemma drinking advocates of bygone days routinely exploited to hush-hush abstinence advocacy. Given the aggressive approach of the pastor above, drinking advocates now appear no longer to need our missionaries' rugged terrain and excruciating challenges in cross-cultural evangelism to exploit to their advantage. Instead proactively initiating the consumption of alcohol to create an accepting climate to present the Gospel appears to be the order of the day.

One can add to this the relatively high number of well-trafficked Baptist blogs that routinely accuse those who embrace abstinence of being "pharisaical legalists" holding to "traditions" while denying "scriptural sufficiency." Who do we think frequents these blogs? Let's say that most of the traffic to popular Southern Baptist blogs are not considered what some call the "graying" of the convention. Indeed Baptist blogs are filled with the youngest among us.

The Conservative Resurgence and the approaching crisis

The **Conservative Resurgence,** which officially began in 1979, made history by turning the theological clock backward to its rightful, biblically authoritative moorings after theological **liberals** and **moderates** alike had tinkered with our theological mainspring and run the hands forward to questionable theological modernity based on rational, anti-supernaturalism. Such subtle neo-orthodox sabotage predictably stripped the screws in Southern Baptist life and painfully revealed the battle over biblical authority we experienced. Southern Baptists lent their ears to her prophets and addressed the crisis head-on. They did what other modern Christian denominations failed to do—*they set their theological clocks to the Almighty's exclusive standard: The Word of God.*

Southern Baptists once again should heed the times*: just beyond the horizon, another approaching crisis awaits our convention.* Before it was biblical belief—*especially belief about the Bible itself*—we stood to lose. We answered modernity's challenge with a "thus saith the Lord." The approaching crisis just ahead is exceedingly more subtle and is wrapped in bright, colorful garments yet is no less a dangerous threat to Southern Baptists. It is not a crisis of *belief* per se, though it is undeniably connected to belief. Nor is it modernity's rationalism, which, as before, stood as the doorkeeper to biblical authority with which our former crisis contended.

Instead the approaching crisis for Southern Baptists concerns *behavior—a cataclysmic moral shift away from biblical holiness expressed in biblical Lordship,* toward the relativistic, **postmodern** norms of American pop culture, including its hedonistic obsession with fulfilling desires. Before, the challenge concerned *doctrine*; the question was, "What do we believe?" The impending crisis Southern Baptists face concerns *discipleship;* the question is, "How will we behave?" The old prophets of Modernity imposed rationalism on the text of biblical revelation; they served to us an *unholy Bible*. The approaching crisis threatens a relativistic ethic that shouts to us *unholy behavior*.

Make no mistake: the popular, trendy appeal for Bible studies in bars; pastors leading men's groups at cigar shops to puff, preach, and partake; conference speakers who openly drink alcohol nevertheless are invited to college campuses as they carve out yet more influence into the youngest generation of Southern Baptists—all this makes an impending moral crisis among Southern Baptists predictably certain.

Indeed—if the current trend to deny total abstinence as the public moral position on consuming alcoholic beverages succeeds—we may not be premature in predicting that the largest Protestant voice for abstinence soon will succumb to the ominous lure of an age of indulgence. We will forfeit our biblical heritage to the whims of an obsessive pop morality that wildly sniffs the wind but for the faintest scent of pleasure fulfilled. If this so-called Christian hedonism, that bases its inner instincts on sensuality and sensuality's ultimate satisfaction succeeds, we lose our children, if possible, to even more extreme versions. Presently the ethical distinction between our flirting with recreationally consuming alcoholic beverages and full **antinomianism** is morally paper-thin. If such distinction vanishes—and inevitably it will—the moral collapse of the Southern Baptist Convention soon could be on us.

The legitimacy of such a position—*that is, total abstinence from alcoholic substances for recreational use*—is the case I hope to make in the remainder of this book. I will marshal history, moral reasoning, and, of course, Scripture—the inerrant Word—to do so.

Let us take a brief detour into a historic era—a place in our cultural timeline about which most of us have heard but too few of us understand: The **Prohibition Era**.

Part 1

Chapter 3

Prohibition Revisited

From 1919 to 1933 our country attempted to enforce prohibition of the manufacture, distribution, and sale of intoxicating beverages across America. When the constitutional amendment was passed, it was hailed as a new era of Christian democracy—a defeat to the destructive effects on faith, family, and culture the alcohol industry had become.

A mere 15 years later, when the 18th Amendment was repealed by the 21st Amendment, a similar excitement existed. It predicted a new era of Christian democracy—a pronounced freedom from tyranny of governmental control. Since 1933 the Prohibition era has become every **libertine**'s whipping post. All one needs to do is mention laws against liquor, stand back, and watch the fireworks begin! We hear such expressions as—

"Remember Prohibition. It didn't work then and it won't work now!"

"You can't legislate morality!"

"Banning alcoholic beverages will drive drinkers undercover, not under conviction!"

"You can't force people to live right!"

These are only a few of the inevitable responses one hears when the Prohibition era is mentioned.

The reader can relax; this is not a book about Prohibition. My goal presently focuses on personal piety and not on public policy. My intention is to make a moral case for personal abstinence from intoxicating substances for recreational purposes. The role individual abstinence plays in imposing itself on the public at large—that is, enacting Prohibition—remains an interesting question. However, probing Prohibition also is an exploration that would steer us far away from my stated focus. Even so, I'd like to mention a few things about Prohibition before I move on.

The Prohibition era

Thinking of Prohibition without thinking of Al Capone is almost impossible. The king of the Chicago underworld made his wealth selling illegal liquor. And, while one can commonly assume men like Capone were an inevitable result of prohibition laws, not all agree with such popular notions. Capone fought over cash, not the right to imbibe alcohol (Editorial, 1947). To be remembered, however, is the fact that laws against cocaine also produce the "inevitable" result of drug cartels today. Hence, just because laws spawn criminals, we are neither reasonable nor biblical if we question law based on consequences alone. Instead, law is to be based on what is right and just.

As I mentioned earlier, conventional wisdom dictates dubbing Prohibition a *national disaster* and a *complete failure*. Nor is conventional wisdom void of scholarly analysis. Finding our social implosion during Prohibition blamed exclusively on Prohibition remains relatively easy. One clinical psychologist, for example, who writes on the social history of alcoholism in America portrays Prohibition similarly to the way we routinely see it visualized in pop culture: "The prohibition struggle itself became more divisive and nativistic: it was heavily rural and Protestant, antiforeigner and anti-Catholic . . . Prohibition was repealed in 1933, and the idea that we should prohibit the sale, production, and use of alcohol disappeared from the American scene [becoming] evident that Prohibition had failed to transform American Society in the monumental way Billy Sunday and other temperance advocates predicted" (Peele, 1989).

Know, however, conventional wisdom's proven track

record of being wrong many times trumps drawing conclusions prematurely. More recently social historians have raised questions about Prohibition's alleged failure and posed serious, scholarly challenges to a once-foregone conclusion. Thus, the popular notion about Prohibition being a colossal failure remains an open question. For example, two eminent sociologists write, "Today the common wisdom, enshrined in many undergraduate textbooks, it [sic] that prohibition was an experiment that failed—it was, in Alston Turk's (1969) words, a 'classic fiasco'. Moreover, proponents of the legalization of drugs who argue that this is the only solution to the problem, constantly cite the failure of prohibition. But, as we shall see, much of the 'failure' of prohibition can be attributed to the fact that it was never completely tried" (Rodney Stark, William Sims Bainbridge, 1997). Stark and Bainbridge argue among other things, that the federal government itself was to blame for much of Prohibition's failure.

Noted theologian and evangelical ethicist Norman Geisler, along with co-author Frank Turek, describe the pre-Prohibition era in troublesome terms: "In the 1830s, with whiskey considered legal tender, annual per capita consumption of hard alcohol (i.e., 80 proof whiskey) reached a staggering 7.1 gallons. In some cases, even preachers were "paid" with whiskey! Alcoholism and its related problems—crime, family violence, incompetence in shops and factories, gambling, etc.—became so troublesome between 1820 and 1850, some began to refer to our country as the 'Alcoholic Republic'. This prompted politicians such as Thomas Jefferson, James Madison, and, later, Abraham Lincoln to urge abstinence for the good of family and country" (Norman Geisler, Frank Turek, 1998).

Furthermore, contrary to those who argue Prohibition's failure, the consumption of alcohol during the Prohibition years decreased in dramatic proportions. Comparing per-capita consumption of alcoholic beverages in 1910 to per-capita consumption in 1934—a year after Prohibition ended—appears to argue for Prohibition's success in reducing alcohol consumption. When the push for Prohibition had reached its zenith in 1910, per-capita consumption stood at approximately 2.6 gallons. When Prohibition ended in 1933, statistics were released a year later on per-capita consumption. The result was staggering: per-capita consumption immediately after Prohibition didn't reach a gallon.

Perhaps the federal government's own study revealed more facts than the whimsical politicians who rushed to rescind Prohibition cared to know. Two years before Prohibition officially ended, a commissioned study given to Congress evaluated the troublesome circumstances Prohibition faced (Wickersham, et al, 1931). Thus, lawmakers were fully aware of Prohibition's enforceability problems. In fact official measures were taken to correct some of the known issues in enforcing Prohibition laws in the Bureau of Prohibition Act, 1927. Even more noteworthy are the recommendations the study made in its conclusions given to Congress in 1931. The first recommendation on the list was a flat-out denial that Prohibition should be repealed: "The Commission is opposed to repeal of the Eighteenth Amendment." Similarly, the Commission asserted its profound opposition toward "the restoration in any manner of the legalized saloon" as well as the "proposal to modify the National Prohibition Act so as to permit manufacture and sale of light wines or beer." In other words, rather than Prohibition's colossal failure, their research concluded Prohibition needed to be revised not rescinded.

Congress heard the counsel given in the study to move forward embracing Prohibition while making adjustments in improving enforcement. The counsel fell on deaf ears, however. Prohibition officially ended December 5, 1933.

The Church, The Temperance Movement, and Prohibition
Before leaving this chapter, let's briefly explore the social climate leading up to the passing of Prohibition in the first

place. We examine this by studying **The Temperance Movement**. No volume of this size possibly could do justice to such a sweeping movement, which not only swallowed the United States but socially saturated many countries around the world. As with *Prohibition*, so with *Temperance*: when the term is mentioned, all varieties of negative images surface.

Many assume the Temperance Movement in this country was nothing more than backward Christian Billy-Bobs bonded together to impose their religious legalism on everybody else. The power of the movement, we are told, was the bully pulpit of persuasive preachers and the tireless efforts of emotionally-driven women's organizations. Concerning the latter, one analysis offers a light-hearted description of the Temperance Movement's most powerful ally—women: *"The eighteenth Amendment . . . came about . . . led largely by sober women fed up with drunk men"* (Norman Geisler, Frank Turek, 1998).

The role of women's groups and their impact on successful passage of Prohibition cannot be overestimated. Undoubtedly they constituted the largest sub-group of social foot-soldiers fighting the liquor industry. If feminists today were half as resolved in their passion for social transformation as were the Temperance women, men beware!

Nor can we say that no truth exists concerning the powerful impact evangelical preaching delivered in the time leading up to Prohibition. For example converted baseball player Billy Sunday not only is known for his fiery revival preaching, with hundreds of thousands "hitting the sawdust trail" professing Christ, notable also was his profoundly effective Prohibition preaching (Timberlake, 1963). Sunday was invariably known as the "the sworn, eternal, and uncompromising enemy of the liquor traffic" as he preached his "booze sermon" all over America.

For instance in 1915 on a single Sabbath afternoon alone, two assemblies totaling 15,000 men showed up to hear Sunday's "booze sermon." At the altar call virtually every man attending both services rushed forward. They vowed themselves to personal abstinence and pledged support for Prohibition. The now-waning Promise Keepers gatherings—men joining together for Christian inspiration—had, even in the group's zenith, nothing compared to Sunday's Prohibition rallies.

While women's groups and persuasive preaching by charismatic men had major input leading to enacting Prohibition, the most neglected machinery—and arguably the most significant machinery—producing the social energy to get Prohibition endorsed was *academia*. The think-tank behind Prohibition was not filled with Bubbas from south Georgia. Instead university presidents, seminary professors, medical professionals, linguists, Classics scholars, and New Testament and Old Testament theologians and scholars alike argued tirelessly in professional journals, books, pamphlets, and speeches not only the *personal virtue* of abstaining from intoxicating beverages but also the *public vice* of manufacturing, distributing, selling, and consuming alcoholic beverages for social and recreational purposes (virtually all temperance advocates supported medicinal alcohol).

Make no mistake: not everyone in the academic world agreed with Temperance advocates. Nonetheless as the culture successfully marched forward toward legalizing social Prohibition, to suggest that abstinence from recreational use of alcoholic intoxicants lacked scholarly support from the academic community in 19th-century America, is or would seem to be blatant ignorance to the historical record or blind captivity to a desired lifestyle. No in-between appears noteworthy.

And, while junk literature on abstinence and Prohibition written by bogus *"experts"* unfortunately existed, one need only pursue the academic literature of that era to be stunned by the magnitude of scholarship behind the idea of abstinence from addictive intoxicants. For our purposes the illustrations below are exclusive to our subject matter.

Eliphalet Nott was born June 25, 1773, in Ashford, CT, to a farming family (Schenectady County, New York History and Genealogy, 1938). Not content to work by the sweat of his brow the young Nott excelled in studies beyond anyone's wildest dreams. In 1795 he enrolled at Brown University (known then as Rhode Island College). On the entrance exam he impressed the faculty so much, he actually qualified for the B.A. degree.

Because of policy strictures he could not receive the honors, however. Working around the policy the faculty prepared yet another exam that he passed. Consequently, the faculty in the fall of the same year bestowed upon him the M.A. degree. At such a young age Nott demonstrated the capability God gave him in academic acumen. Indeed he would pour out his life as an academician.

Three years later Mr. Nott was appointed as pastor of the prestigious First Presbyterian Church of Albany, NY. Here he rubbed shoulders with many post-revolutionary politicians. Because others almost immediately observed his intellectual prowess, Nott was sought not only as co-chaplain of the New York state legislature but also as trustee of Union College in Schenectady, over which, in 1804, he became president and remained so for 62 years. At that time Union was the third-largest university and was surpassed only by Harvard and Yale.

Note the following quote from Eliphalet Nott. Remember: Nott was an accomplished scholar in Latin, Greek, and Hebrew. For his entire life he was thoroughly given to scholarly pursuits and for 62 years remained as president of one of the leading universities of his day. Contextually the quote is found as Nott nails his platform in place to argue his case for abstinence. He builds on the Word of God.

He wrote, "Far be it from me to promulgate or defend opinions contrary to the announcements of the Bible. The Bible is at once the unerring standard of faith, as well as the authoritative rule of life . . . [the disciple] attends to its several announcements as so many oracles from heaven, and surrendering all his pride and all his prepossessions says from the bottom of his heart, as he turns its hallowed pages: 'Speak Lord, for thy servant heareth' . . . We may err in our interpretations of the language of the Bible, but the Bible itself never errs; and in nothing, as is believed, has its import been more misapprehended than in the countenance it has some times been supposed to give to the use of intoxicating liquors as a beverage . . . But if the ultimate appeal for the decision [concerning abstinence] is to the Bible, how can it be considered any longer an open question; for in that case what room is there even for debate?" (Nott, 1857).

Now admittedly Eliphalet Nott could be wrong, his scholarship inadequate, his science bad, his historiography skewed, and his hermeneutics flawed—even after 62 years as president of the third-largest academic institution in 19th-century America. Granted. But let us not insult him by suggesting he was an uneducated, biblically illiterate *moral legalist* who imposed *tradition-driven* preference when he so clearly argued his case from unerring biblical revelation. *To do so, in my view, reveals ever so plainly who the real tradition-driven people are.*

Did Eliphalet Nott stand alone? Was he eccentric in his view? He was not. In fact he stood on biblical abstinence with many giants in the academic world at that time.

George Whitefield Samson was born September 29, 1819, at Harvard, MA. His father, Abisha Samson, was the sixth in descent from Abraham Samson, who arrived at Plymouth among the earliest Pilgrims; and his mother, Mehetable Kenrick, was the sixth in descent from one of the earliest Puritan settlers at Boston (*GW Magazine*, 2009). According to William Cathcart, before he was 13-years old, he became highly familiar with the most scholarly biblical commentaries available of the day (Cathcart, 1881).

Samson entered Brown University in 1835 and studied under the famed Baptist, Francis Wayland, until 1839. Shortly after graduating, he enrolled at Newton Theological Seminary. Receiving a degree from Newton in 1843, and after serving several Baptist churches as pastor along the way and teaching in several schools, Dr. Samson was invited to become fifth president of Columbian College, Washington, DC, in 1859. He remained there all through the Civil War years (today, this is George Washington University).

Also Dr. Samson was associated with the boards of the Northern and the Southern Baptist organizations. He served as trustee of the Southern Baptist Theological Seminary at Greenville, SC. Perhaps Cathcart made the best statement about Dr. Samson when he said, "No Baptist clergyman in the country is perhaps better known throughout the denomination than Dr. Samson."

Although he was not a prolific writer, President Samson left his academic mark on both the academy at large and learned Baptist thinking in particular. One major work by Dr. Samson dealt with the elements of art critique. However, by far the greatest achievement Dr. Samson left for his Baptist descendants is a work all but forgotten now. According to Cathcart, at the request of two Conventions Dr. Samson published in 1885, a treatise entitled "Divine Law As to Wines" about wine in religious uses. This volume of mammoth proportions takes the reader through a virtually exhaustive look at wine in history, both profane and religious, with an obvious focus on wine in the Scriptures of the Old and New Testaments.

Writing in the same vein as other temperance theologians Dr. Samson takes the moderation advocates to the historical, theological, and biblical woodshed. With not an ounce less confidence than Eliphalet Nott did Dr. Samson put forth the unpopular thesis—at least unpopular in today's atmosphere among many Baptists—indicating biblical revelation knows of no such sanction of alcoholic beverages for pleasurable purposes as moderation advocates maintain.

Indeed, if moderation is needed, it is needed for the wine God approves. No such moderation is called for concerning the wine God condemns; for the wine God does not approve solicits from us one single response: *abstinence.*

Thus far we've briefly considered from academia a Presbyterian and a Baptist who were renowned not for their ability to whip up emotions from the masses through their rhetorical skills in the pulpit. Instead they were known for their academic achievements among scholars. Let's round it out nicely with a Methodist.

In 1882 New Testament scholar, Leon C. Field, penned a series of articles for *The Methodist Quarterly* collected and published the following year by Phillips & Hunt, New York under one title: *Oinos: A Discussion of the Bible Wine Question.* So influential within the scholarly community was this volume that the journal of *The New Hampshire Annual Conference* characterized Field's work as "*a masterly and exhaustive argument on the subject, which has never been overthrown and which has elicited favorable comment by the best minds on both sides of the Atlantic*" (Tait, N/D). Later on in this volume I intend to utilize some of Field's material.

Were Baptists, Presbyterians, and Methodists the only academic communities that argued biblically, theologically, and ethically the case for abstinence from intoxicating drink? Far from it. Timothy Dwight, president of Yale, caused no small unsettling in his New Haven academic circle not for lecturing against intemperance but against temperance drinking. In other words, he embraced absolute abstinence (Knout, 1925).

Frederic Richard Lees, British theologian, philosopher, and Old Testament scholar, literally shook England with his sophisticated understanding of abstinence. He was widely and derisively known as the "Ghost of Temperance" because of his frail, thin physique (Bank, 1892). Yet he was feared all

England over for his forceful, merciless bouts in debates with liquor advocates. Lee's astute scholarship is most visible with his mammoth production, *The Temperance Bible Commentary* (1870). Co-authored with Dawson Burns, the Temperance Commentary was widely hailed as a single but exhaustive volume for the study of wine in the Bible and a virtual masterpiece that thoroughly explores every biblical passage which mentioned wine.

Both time and space fail to exhaust the period when academic scholarship, though not unanimous, nonetheless impressively stood behind evangelicalism's insistence on abstinence from intoxicants for recreational use. The names include Charles Spurgeon, John L. Dagg, John Broadus, William Ritchie, Francis Wayland, Moses Stuart, Taylor Lewis, Lyman Beecher—and the list simply could run on.

Given such a great cloud of witnesses we are not surprised that entire Christian denominations were convinced of biblical abstinence. In fact virtually every Protestant denomination offered public pro-abstinent statements. Yet today people commonly argue that adhering to abstinence is mostly, if not entirely, indicative of uneducated preachers who possess an eerie, obsessive focus on a few moral taboos such as drinking, dancing, dealing cards, and smoking cigarettes. The facts say otherwise.

Most evangelical denominations were solidly behind temperance reform. Many denominations gave large sums of money for temperance education. Furthermore, according to Timberlake, liberal Christianity strongly advocated temperance reform (Timberlake, 1963).

Notable liberal Baptist theologian Walter Rauschenbusch, who, more than anyone else, fathered what ultimately was called the "Social Gospel", fully embraced the temperance movement. He wrote, "Alcohol is a spirit born of hell [but it is] merely a satellite and tool of a greater devil, and that devil is Mammon" (Knout, 1925). Who then would be surprised to learn that urban Christianity, the demographic seedbed for social gospel faith, was as much a part of the temperance movement as was rural Christianity?

In 1906 reports said the most urbanized religious group of all faiths were Christian Scientists, who had more than 82 percent of their members residing in urban America. Yet Christian Scientists were among the fiercest apologists of total abstinence and Prohibition. In addition Unitarians were similar in demographic makeup; they too strongly advocated abstinence from alcoholic beverages for recreational purposes.

Conclusion

As we sum up our brief journey through history, let's recap a few lessons we've learned.

• First, the passage of legal Prohibition did not take the country by surprise. For a generation the forces behind Prohibition were zealously at work converting the masses.

• Second, the forces that led to the legalized ban of intoxicating beverages were a mixture of pop cultural influences blended with an overwhelming stockpile of support from academia. In addition some of the best and brightest biblical scholars argued tirelessly and unambiguously for abstinence based primarily on biblical revelation coupled with indisputable moral reasoning.

• Third, while the evangelical church produced an unusual amount of support for abstinence from intoxicants, emerging from both the popular grassroots sector and the academic world, we mistakenly assume that evangelicals were alone in their insistence on abstinence. Instead an amazing alliance forged from conservative to liberal—from Christian Scientists to Unitarians—all bonded together to legalize Prohibition.

• Fourth, whatever conclusion we draw from the Prohibition experiment, we would be both ill-founded and illegitimate to conclude Prohibition a grand, colossal failure.

Part 2

Chapter 4

Sizing Up the Options: Five Views on Drinking Alcohol

A Brief Look at What We've Said

Let's summarize what, up to this point, we've studied. First, I've been as honest as I know how to be about why this book needed to be written. Alcohol destroys. In some ways it is like a parasite that slowly but steadily saturates an organism and gobbles up every morsel of life. Sometimes alcohol is acid which, on contact with the unwary, immediately mutilates and so twists one's life that no hope exists to undo its disastrous effects on family, vocation, self-image, and faith. For me this is not abstract; it is reality—what I personally experienced in my own rendezvous with this dangerous drug—albeit many years ago.

Thus on the one hand this book is a public confessional—the words of a former drunk peeling back the dingy pages of his torn, scarred life, a large part of which resulted from his unfortunate, uncontrollable binge with beer, bottled wine, and bourbon-on-the-rocks. Yet on the other hand it is the triumphant testimony of a man—a gutter man, a hopeless man, a helpless man—rescued from himself, his sin, and his addiction. While I was drowning in a sea of intoxicating substances, the God of heaven pitched to me His rope of rescue and pulled me to the shore of grace. From grace's shore I continue to drink—not from the bottles of counterfeit beauty I once found attractive. Instead I drink from the fountain of life found only through faith in the Son of God, the Lord Jesus Christ.

Second, we looked briefly at the shift in both attitude and belief the Evangelical church as well as other religious bodies have experienced during the past century and half. And while the church has not been unanimous in its understanding of beverage drinks containing alcoholic substances, nevertheless a strong thread of abstinence from intoxicants beginning in the first-century church can easily be traced. Even more, the aged, mature church gave blossom to its full flower of abstinence in the 19th century. Indeed the temperance theologians viewed themselves as nothing less than reformers who, in the spirit of Luther, Calvin, Zwingli, and Hubmaier, once again were capturing the essence of biblical revelation.

However, whereas the aforementioned reformers concerned themselves with justification by faith alone, those arguing for abstinence from intoxicating substances defended a lesser though significant biblical teaching. The former focused on precisely how one becomes rightly related with God. The latter focused not only on how a believer who is rightly related to God lives but also on how the church informs culture and ultimately transforms culture. Theologians and biblical scholars who argued tirelessly for moral abstinence from intoxicating beverages were informing culture to transform culture. Just as the divine right of kings was finally overthrown through consistent, corrective interpretation of biblical truth, so the church passed through its darkened stupor of accepting as biblical fact the selling of human souls as so much chattel property. Thus abolition was born!

No better illustration of this sense of reformation surfaces than from 19th-century New Testament scholar Leon C. Field's contribution to abstinence teachings (Field, 1883). After rehearsing the church's embarrassing reluctance to rightly usurp both the divine right of kings and the human right to own humans Field exhorts: "The old lesson must once more be learned, that a traditional interpretation of Scripture is not conclusive proof of any doctrine, but is often an obscuration of the truth of God. It is needful, therefore, to pray against that bias which, by importing its own foregone conclusions into the word of Scripture, and, by refusing to acknowledge what makes against its own prejudices, has proved the greatest hindrance to all fair interpretation, and has tended, more than anything else in the world, to check the free course of divine truth." For Field, along with the majority of 19th-century evangelical Protestantism, Scripture reveals the liberty of every human soul as a God-endowed right, but such liberty does not include the liberty to self-destruct by poisoning, through intoxicating substances, either one's soul or one's society. The Bible affirms abolition from slavery; so too, the Bible affirms abstinence from intoxicants.

The shift in thinking that led to legalized Prohibition cannot be described as a sudden change of heart. Instead the temperance movement lasted a full hundred years or more. It possessed far-reaching results from academia to the city street. What intellectuals were teaching in higher education, popular preachers and massive armies of foot-soldiers, both male and female, took deeply into the jungles of depraved, alcohol-soaked society and insisted on abstinence from the demon brew. Nor was the passion for truth and Christian civility wasted on a lost cause. Former U.S. Health and Welfare Secretary Joseph Califano wrote: "During prohibition, admission to mental health institutions for alcoholic psychosis dropped 60 percent; arrests for drunk and disorderly conduct went down 50 percent; welfare agencies reported significant declines in cases due to alcohol-related family problems, and the death rate from impure alcohol did not rise. Nor did Prohibition generate a crime wave. Homicide increased at a higher rate between 1900 and 1910 than during Prohibition, and organized crime was well established in the cities before 1920" (Califano, 1996).

Mapping out where we're going

The next several chapters, which constitute Part 2, are brief. Nevertheless the content could prove challenging. We'll be looking in condensed form at the field of Christian **ethics**. For many of us studying ethics is a fairly rigorous challenge. Indeed ethics usually is considered optional in undergraduate study and, in many cases, is rarely emphasized in seminary education. In fact when I attended both Bible school and seminary, courses in ethics were widely considered by the student body as necessary evils. Most of us wanted evangelism, biblical exposition, and theology. Ethics was placed in the same category as Church Administration 101. Surely neither ethics nor administration would win one soul to Christ! However, the fact that both were highly necessary to being an effective pastor in God's church was freshly demonstrated to me later.

Thus, while the chapters are only introductory, I trust them to be helpful. And, if the content appears challenging, will it not be enough to suggest sometimes getting to the truth of the matter—including the truth of biblical revelation, and specifically in this case, whether for believers to use intoxicating substances for recreational use is morally acceptable—IS challenging?

Such recognition of the challenge before us makes me recall something that desperately needs to be said about the believer's use of intoxicating substances. Listen but a moment to the song sung by advocates for the pleasurable use of alcohol. The simplistic refrain continues its melody, "The Bible nowhere says, 'thou shalt not drink alcohol.'" Or, another chorus lifted to heights barely short of the Spirit's inspiration Himself is the tune sung often by pastors themselves entitled, "Jesus turned the water into wine." Such simplistic, inadequate, and unstudied conclusions boldly pronounced by preachers of the Book without one shred of argument pertaining to imbibing intoxicating substances for pleasurable use remains frightening for the church, not to mention culture. It also demonstrates—quite nicely in fact—a sure reason to study ethics, ever how challenging the study may be.

Over the next five chapters we'll briefly explain and evaluate five views commonly taken on recreationally consuming intoxicating substances. We'll begin with what may be described as the most passive view—no restraint at all for imbibing intoxicants. Moving on, we'll continue across the moral continuum to the most restrictive of all—*total abstinence*. By now the reader should not be surprised at the view I will argue as most consistent with biblical revelation and moral reason—that of total abstinence in an age of indulgence.

Part 2

Chapter 5

Drink, Drank, Drunk:
"And the Problem Is?"

We now begin our journey in understanding varying positions on consuming intoxicating substances for recreational purposes. We believe five views exist. Our first step is in liberty's direction. By liberty I mean neither political liberty nor religious liberty *per se*. Instead I mean without moral restraint—without the pesky little creature whose razor-sharp teeth draw blood when we act or think against conscience. Such a creature God Himself custom-designed to dwell in every human being. Thus, we learn what culture without conscience contributes to community life, the contribution of which may be summed up in a single word —*hedonism*— hedonism as it specifically relates to consuming intoxicating drink.

Hedonism described

The reader will recall the college president about which I spoke in chapter one. The image of this middle-aged man happily pouring from a beer keg into the mouth of the young college coed the intoxicating foam marks the quintessential understanding of today's pop culture about alcohol. For them consuming intoxicants is a right—a received expectation to fulfill without hindrance or obstacle any desire that assures the most pleasure and avoids the most pain. In short, it is the age-old philosophy of **hedonism** perched under an American flag.

The real tragedy points to hedonistic people such as our college administrator who possesses the public's trust. Yet without moral restraint such hedonists perpetuate an endless pleasure-island ethic by promoting *drink, drank, and drunk* to our children—my children . . .your children . . ..

Nor is this the only example of elite educators lobbying for the consumption of intoxicants. Despite the pronouncement of the chairman of the National Transportation Safety Board, who recently said, "State Age-21 laws are one of the most effective public policies ever implemented in the Nation" (Wechsler, 2008), several university administrators in July 2008 forged an alliance dubbed the "Amethyst Initiative", which focuses on lowering the legal drinking age to 18. Presently the initiative is backed by 100+ university administrators, some of whom hold "town-hall" meetings around the country to stir up support for their cause.

The obvious presumption driving the efforts of the Amethyst Initiative is that drinking poses to our offspring no serious threat either physically or emotionally. Of course the fact that younger-aged drinking most probably undermines both our children's moral development and their spiritual senses appears not to concern in the least these highly motivated educators.

Nonetheless the bare thought of stemming drunkenness among 21-year olds by inviting openly—and if they have their way, legally—millions on millions of first-year students to the campus pub party is too ridiculous for words. A known universal is that even if we'd grant their assumption—that is, the assumption that lowering the drinking age would curb binge drinking and drunkenness among college seniors—as profoundly ridiculous as it is, such age-lowering most likely would result in millions of first-year students, desperately hoping to connect with their upper-class fellows, happily taking their place around the bar to prove themselves worthy of acceptance and association. As the worn but relevant cliché asks, from what planet were these educated people plucked?

Elite hedonists positioned as university administrators pledging to the public that if we'll send them our children, our children will be rewarded with a stellar education about which we will be proud, remind one more and more of a clever ponzi scheme that promises unwary investors exceptional profits if they would but place their cash into ponzi care. Such actions and assumptions of these elite educators represent hedonism in all its rich and interesting colors.

Additionally while hedonists have plenty of spark to indulge, they apparently lack the slightest potential to infer. Are they not aware that transition from high school to college cuts the widest canyon of increased consumption of intoxicating beverages among our young, especially among young women? Moreover, do only the non-elite know the secret that the younger a female is when she first imbibes, the more likely she will be to consume intoxicants throughout her life? Says Jon Morgenstern, professor of psychiatry and vice-president at the National Center on Addiction and Substance Abuse: "College campuses are the place where drinking norms are set for educated individuals . . .. The rate of drinking is astronomical. College is really a training ground for becoming an alcoholic" (Morris A., 2008).

Nor did they blink when Tim Marchell, director of Gannett Health Services, indicated national fatalities are reduced by 11 percent because of the older legal drinking age. He concluded, "The scientific evidence is compelling." Allen Bova, director of Risk Management and Insurance, joins in the discussion and confidently asserts, "Every death, every sexual assault, confirms that opinion that students under 21 should not consume alcohol" (Falk, 2008).

In the face of such indisputable odds, the Amethyst Initiative nonetheless marches toward its twisted sense of pleasure-driven utopia where insatiable desires of limitless liquor expressed by the youngest and most vulnerable among us shall not go unheeded. After all, why should they care? Our sons and daughters—not theirs—are the ones bloated with beer, bourbon, and bottles of wine.

Given the tragic scenario above, parents could find at least some relief knowing they had kindergarten through high school to sharpen the blades of their children's moral sense before those children reach the moment in their lives in which the resistance to intoxicants hits them full force. Unfortunately any relief parents might feel in escaping the octopus reach of secular hedonism is but a deceptive illusion which, if parents fail to grasp, will surely morph to a deadly one. Make no mistake: like burnt oil on beautiful concrete, the libertine spirit of hedonism, focusing on the pleasure ethic alone, seeps deeply into the porous surface of our society and finds no limits to its ugly, scarring stain.

British researchers know too well the stubborn stains indicative of hedonism's irrational quest for raw pleasure. Parents in Great Britain find themselves scrambling to understand and counter the most recent trends of their precious offspring as their thirsts for alcohol spiral dangerously out of control. Once again young females pose the greatest challenge. Research shows British female teens start drinking an average of two years younger than women who now are in their mid-20s did, with most admitting to consuming alcohol by the age of 13 or 14 (Devlin, 2009).

Valerie McMunn, University of Manchester, who led the study, noted "Women are commencing drinking at an earlier age and are experiencing the negative consequences of alcohol but show no activity to curb this activity . . . The negative aspects of their behavior puts their sexual, physical, and psychological health at risk." Some of the complications noted were unprotected sex, getting into cars with strange men, and even seeing their friends fall asleep on roundabouts after a night of imbibing. By far the most frightening, doctors warned, was research showing that drinking from a younger age leads teen-agers to go on to consume alcohol more heavily. In addition the medical community sounded the alarm that accelerated drinking habits are leading to a record number of young women with liver problems: "[Medical researchers] say that they are seeing increasing numbers of women in their 20s and 30s with cirrhosis of the liver, a disease virtually unheard of in that age group a decade ago."

So much for gaining a picture of unchecked hedonism's contribution in understanding our age of indulgence. But exactly what is hedonism?

Hedonism defined

If we but took the word *hedonism* itself, we could conclude none other than hedonism, strictly speaking, is concerned only with pleasure. The Greek root *hedone* literally means "pleasure." The term *ism* often finds itself riding the coattails of other terms with the decided effect of changing those terms into theories, practices, philosophies, and even obsessions. Someone quipped that we live in a world of innumerable *isms*. Hence hedonism is primarily a theory, a philosophy, but most of all an obsession with pleasure.

Epicurus, sometimes labeled hedonism's founder, was born in Athens, Greece (circa 342 B.C.). The Epicurean community we find in the New Testament era stemmed from the fourth century B.C. A full 400 years later Epicurus' descendants, not having ditched their master's desire for pleasure, are intellectually sparring with the Apostle Paul: *Now while Paul waited for them [Silas and Timothy] at Athens, his spirit was stirred in him, when he saw the city wholly given to idolatry . . . Then certain philosophers of the Epicureans, and of the Stoicks, encountered him. And some said, What will this babbler say? other some, He seemeth to be a setter forth of strange gods: because he preached unto them Jesus, and the resurrection. And they took him, and brought him unto Areopagus, saying, May we know what this new doctrine, whereof thou speakest, is? For thou bringest certain strange things to our ears: we would know therefore what these things mean (Acts 17:16-20).*
58

Apart from the resurrection of Jesus would other concerns be raised between Paul and the Epicureans? Indeed many issues exist, according to Scripture. Even Luke's description of Paul's enlightening walk through the streets hints at it, for the city is *wholly given to idolatry.*

Paul feels a chilled, pronounced loneliness as he waits for his comrades (1 Thess. 3:1). Strolling the streets he cannot help his mind racing back to the prestigious days of this historic city. Athens was the arts centre of the ancient world. Here philosophy's magnetic trio—Socrates, Plato, and Aristotle—sold their intellectual wares to willing disciples. Not only was the Academy of Plato situated in Athens, but the Garden of Epicurus also was there. In Epicurus' thought, the controlling center around which all of life revolved concerned pleasure. For him what promises the maximal pleasure and the minimum pain essentially defines What is the good? What is the moral? and What is the right? (Norman L. Geisler, Paul D. Feinberg, 1980).

The historian Pliny stated during Nero's reign that Athens had in excess of 30,000 public statues, not counting the statues people kept in their private homes! Another historian quipped that finding a god rather than a man in Athens was easier. No surprise Luke describes Paul's reaction as *his spirit stirred within.* Furthermore the sheer magnitude of statues found in Athens perfectly illustrates the epicurean spirit—abundance, limitlessness, and, of course, *pleasure.*

In short, hedonism is about pleasure and our hopeless addiction in chasing its skirt. But mentioning such immediately begs the question—pleasure for what? Well, anything that fills your cup, that's what. The fact is, the content of pleasure is open for discussion among hedonists themselves. In other words hedonism appears in many colors, sizes, shapes, and forms. One hedonist may obsess himself or herself for raptures of sexual delight. A quick mind flash shines brightly on the name *Hugh Hefner* and the Playboy Mansion. But for purposes here we apply the pleasure principle to the issue of consuming intoxicating substances. In doing so we find ourselves face to face with pop culture's insatiable thirst for the legalized drug. Happy Hour captures hedonism's quintessential spirit. Just drink, I say! Drink, man! Drink! For tomorrow we die.

Hedonism debunked

One of the persistent problems about which those who study ethics are aware concerns absolutes. Do moral absolutes exist? If so, can we know them? Some have gone so far as to say the only thing that does not change is change itself. Others reply, if all things change, how can we possibly know change without an absolute standard by which to measure change? Geisler and Feinberg define what we mean by a *universal, moral absolute*: "By a *universal* right is meant a duty that is binding on *all men at all times and in all places*." Is your head spinning? So is mine. Let's move on for now, with the understanding we may revisit this again.

Debunking hedonism begins with understanding that the pleasure principle is a form of **ethical relativism**. Basically ethical relativism reduces to the principle indicating the absence of moral absolutes. In 1987 University of Chicago professor Allan Bloom wrote a devastating critique of American culture, particularly academia. He said, "There is one thing a professor can be absolutely certain of: almost every student entering the university believes, or says he believes, that truth is relative. If this belief is put to the test, one can count on the students' reaction: they will be uncomprehending. That anyone should regard the proposition as not self-evident astonishes them, as though he were calling into question 2+2=4" (Bloom, 1987). Bloom couldn't have been more prophetic of the so-called **postmodern** mindset saturating our culture if he'd tried, for postmodernity swims comfortably within a pool where no absolutes are allowed.

Perhaps the most popular expression of relativism is captured in the practical moral guide, "What's true for you is not necessarily true for me." Such ambiguous nonsense makes morals reduce to personal tastes: I like vanilla; you like chocolate. Two ethicists write, "When morality is reduced to personal tastes, people exchange the moral question, What is good? for the pleasure question, What feels good? They assert their desires and then attempt to rationalize their choices with moral language. In this case, the tail wags the dog. Instead of morality constraining pleasures . . . The pleasures define morality. This effort at ethical decision-making is really nothing more than thinly veiled self-interest—pleasure as ethics" (Francis J. Beckwith, Gregory Koukl, 1998).

Since we've anchored hedonism securely within ethical relativism, we're in a much better position to offer our critique. *First, hedonism does not deal in moral principle but in personal preference.* It is unconcerned about *moral duty* but about *mere desire.* What happens when one person's desire conflicts with another person's desire? Hedonism defines the good as *pleasure.* Therefore, since the fact that my pleasure fulfilled is good, the other person's desires are absolutely irrelevant.

Second, hedonism wrongly assumes all pleasure is good and all pain is bad. This is questionable at best. Suppose someone received satisfying pleasure from torturing people with hot pokers? If the good is what is personally pleasurable, what normally follows is the concept that torturing people with hot pokers is good. Moreover we must concede that not all pain is bad. If my chest hurts, the pain very well may be a life-saving alarm indicating something obviously is wrong with my heart. In that case the pain ultimately was good for me though it was not pleasurable to me. Thus, the good and the pleasurable cannot be equated.

If hedonism fails at its core—that is, at its central controlling principle, the principle of pleasure—it collapses as a viable moral option. Therefore, consuming intoxicating substances based on the pleasure principle alone collapses. Just because mind-altering drugs relax one's body, renew one's spirit, release one's inhibitions, or relieve one's pain hardly makes the case that consumption of such drugs is morally good.

Conclusion

Our culture is obsessed with both pursuing and fulfilling pleasure. The Hedonistic view of consuming intoxicants fails as a viable moral option for us to consider. Pleasure outstripping all other meaningful moral concerns furthermore is biblically bankrupt. Consequently hedonistic views of imbibing alcoholic beverages or other mind-altering drugs remain morally inappropriate for the believing community. In addition defenses for drinking in moderation—*if the defenses are based on pleasure alone*—are, at minimum, open to serious moral question, since hedonism remains, at its core, morally unacceptable.

Part 2

Chapter 6

"Think Before You Drink"

Our journey through five positions on consuming intoxicating substances began with what we called *hedonism*. Hedonism, according to our moral structure, is obviously the view with the fewest restraints on consuming intoxicants. Arguably hedonists possess not only the fewest restraints but indeed no moral restraints at all. For them the pursuit of the highest good is in their moral framework, with the highest good being pleasure. They consume intoxicants because they *desire* to consume; intoxicants are *satisfying* to consume — *relaxing* to consume. For in consuming intoxicants they gain a euphoric release, an experience from which no other source they've known or found can surpass.

In one sense hedonism is perfectly understandable being the logical deduction of culture without Christ. In another sense, however, evangelical Christians who advocate and/or consume intoxicating substances for pleasure clutch in their palm a curious moral position. For in essence what they appear to suggest is that the desired experiential effects supplied by intoxicating drugs remain unavailable through their relationship with the God of the Bible. *Moral hedonism and historic Christianity are hardly compatible.*

Drinking: let's think about it!

With a bit of background in hedonism we're now in a position to briefly examine another moral position on consuming alcoholic beverages. We've dubbed this position *think before you drink.* Admittedly just the mere pause—that is, "to think" —assumes that one is morally reflecting despite how meager such reflection is. Thus, we have the beginnings of restraint— a moral birth that begs for consideration before one consumes.

In the last chapter we introduced a few terms that are perhaps new to many readers. We now introduce two more terms (remember to consult the glossary for these terms as often as needed): *utilitarianism* and *teleological.* Before we proceed with the definitions, two points for clarity need to be expressed. The first one is short, but the second will need some space.

First, by no stretch am I suggesting that a mere definition of these terms and subsequently applying the definition for our purposes exhausts the meaning and usage of these terms. In many respects entire books could be written—and have been written—on each term respectively. Also the complexities involved hardly get justice in a book such as this present one. Second, one must at least gain a sense of my usage of these terms to grasp the moral case I'm making for total abstinence in an age when sheer indulgence, and in many cases, full moral acceptance and approval decidedly rule.

To guard against the reader's misunderstanding, let me be perfectly clear: *the non-negotiable premise on which any doctrinal belief or moral behavior is constructed ever and always will be the Bible's full and perfect truth—in short, the inerrancy of Scripture.* No extrabiblical author captured the idea of inerrancy quite like Princeton's 19th-century champion, B. B. Warfield: "Whatever Scripture says, God says" (Warfield, 2003). Thus our uncompromising allegiance to God's unerring Word must not be overshadowed by what we now must make equally clear.

Societal development continues to pose challenges to the Christian worldview. Science, technology, and medical advancements, just to name a few, raise questions, including moral questions about which the biblical record does not specifically address. To cite only one example, the moral complexities raised by DNA research, stem-cell research, and so-called "cloning" of both human and nonhuman life are complexities the Bible nowhere specifically addresses. Even uttering the question, "Where in the Bible does it say, 'thou shalt not clone'?", expresses a dead giveaway indicating that no mental energy on serious reflection about the moral complexities involved has been expended. For those content with merely asking such questions instantly relieves them from further consideration. After all, if we can't find a biblical verse to address the moral issue head-on, are we not to presume that believers are free to embrace or are free to not embrace the practice? I have to confess that many in the church are infected with just such a simplistic virus pertaining to moral reasoning.

From my standpoint the position just described reveals two unfortunate mistakes. First, to expect the Bible to directly address every conceivable moral issue is absurd. Not that Scripture does not, *in some way*, address every conceivable moral issue. Rather demanding that Scripture *directly* address them is the profound absurdity (see below).

Another mistake is the assumption that unless Scripture speaks *directly* to a moral problem—as in "thou shalt not clone"—no strong moral case can be constructed. Consequently the Christian worldview, specifically where it addresses moral matters, collapses in on itself. It offers both to church and culture a mangled moral heap that is worthless because it cannot speak to every sphere of life. In short, the interpreter who looks in vain for the "for thou shalt not clone" not only misuses Scripture but also thoroughly ignores Scripture. That person mistakenly concludes that God does not address a significant, moral sphere of life.

What role does the Bible play in writing the complex plot of moral behavior? If the Bible does not *directly* speak to certain issues, how does the Bible *indirectly* speak to them? Two theologians explain: "This issue may appear to concern only non-evangelicals. Typically, they deny that Scripture can be used in ethics, for they see no single ethical system in Scripture, but rather conflicting ethical perspectives from the various authors" (Feinberg & Feinberg, 1993). Non-evangelicals actually have a fairly smooth surface on which to paint as they prepare their moral arguments for today's issues. Given their understanding of Scripture's nature, as containing some truth and some error, they simply can use the Bible as putty and smooth over a tiny crack here or filling in a few holes there. And, if the Bible ever seems to threaten the non-evangelical's rational maturity, it can easily be described as lacking modern pliability and therefore discerned unfit for use. In short, the Bible becomes dismissible.

Interestingly both the evangelical who searches in vain for the "thou shalt not clone" and the non-evangelical who holds to a "some truth, some error" approach to Scripture in the end pursue similar paths. *Albeit for different reasons, both end up rejecting Scripture's authoritative relevancy in addressing every moral sphere of life.* Those of us, however, whose premise is as stated above—inerrancy—pursue no such dead-end street. For us the Bible must always be the moral hub for the moral positions we construct.

Even so, thinking an inerrant Bible ends the matter for us is insufficient. It does not. We do not have to think less because of our unwavering commitment to the biblical text; rather we have to think more. Inspired authority is only the beginning. No guarantee exists for inspired, infallible interpretations. The Feinbergs made clear in a series of questions: Must one who believes all of Scripture keep the Old Testament dietary laws? (Lev. 11). Are we required to build a parapet around our roof so no one will fall off and be killed? (Deut. 22:8). The point we must keep in mind is this: *the Bible presents a definitive perspective on moral behavior, but that does not mean modification is not required to apply the Bible's moral perspective today.*

Finally we need to say that no clearer example exists than the present study to illustrate the necessity of modifying the *application* of biblical truth in constructing a thorough, biblically-driven moral perspective on whether God approves the recreational use of intoxicating substances. The fact is, an ignored and mostly overlooked premise in understanding the issues involved in this discussion is this: the Bible reveals little about virtually every intoxicating substance available today, whether legal or illegal, including distilled liquors, beers, and wines. Does such indicate that the Bible has nothing morally constructive to say about intoxicating substances? It does not. Recall while the Bible may not speak *directly* to any number of moral issues today, it does indeed speak—and speak profoundly—to the moral question of recreationally consuming intoxicating substances, even if it speaks *indirectly*.

Many limit Scripture's authority to addressing whether God approves the recreational use or non-use of "wine." This is a tragic mistake.

First, the "wine" about which the Bible speaks—fermentation aside—is hardly the mass-produced, distilled substances sold exclusively for recreational usage in bars and supermarkets today. And, contrary to what some suggest, whether, contextually, the substance Scripture either commended or condemned is identical to the substances available today really does make a difference. Thus, we must address this possible substance discrepancy. In **Part 3** I intend to focus more on this.

Second, to limit the biblical record's application to simply "wine" or even alcoholic beverages for that matter neglects the much larger and desperately needed application to an endless parade of intoxicants whose primary purpose is identical to "wine"—*stimulating pleasure*. Incidentally, once again we must remind ourselves, unlike the ancients who necessarily consumed grape products specifically for survival, those lobbying for moderately consuming intoxicants today in the form of drinking distilled wines, beers, and other alcoholic beverages are lobbying for consumption distinctively driven by pleasure alone.

Even so, Scripture knows nothing of mind-altering drugs we have today on both open and black markets. Nevertheless we believe biblical revelation speaks definitively—albeit *indirectly*—about them. Furthermore, as we construct our moral position on consuming intoxicating substances, "wine" is simply one of many intoxicants within a conglomeration of substances a biblically driven ethic brands as largely immoral if used for strictly recreational purposes.

Defining terms

Since we've had our little trip around the world, let's explore two definitions. Afterward we will show why we reject the "think-before-you-drink" position. The term **utilitarianism** appears intimidating. Actually for our purposes here the idea is fairly simple. Utilitarianism focuses almost exclusively on results—not just any results but good results. Even more it focuses on not just good results but good results for the greatest number of people. So in essence the moral idea is bringing about the greatest good for the greatest number of people (Cahn & Haber, 1995).

A similar moral idea is couched in the term **teleological**. The word itself originates from a Greek root pointing to the "end design"—the "ultimate purpose." Again the "outcome" or "result" is in focus. What do these terms have to do with the subject we're pursuing? When we examine our culture's moral values, inevitably we find in large part the primary motivation for moral behavior focuses on the end result. Why should children stay in school? To get a good job and make a lot of money. Why should kids not shoot crack? Because crack will fry their brains like they were eggs in a hot pan. Why should kids not have unprotected sex? Because they could get a disease or could ruin their lives with an unwanted pregnancy.

Why should kids not drink and drive? They can have a wreck or hurt somebody else.

The answers above clearly are focused on the *outcome* of the questionable behavior, not the *behavior itself*. In other words, what makes the act wrong is not the doing of it but the consequences of it. Proponents of this concept might say, "Nothing is wrong with having sex. Do it! But please; when you do it, do it responsibly. Wear condoms." A similar thought might be, "Nothing is wrong with drinking nor even getting drunk. Do it! But please; when you do it, do it responsibly. Don't drink and drive. Or, consider your health. Or, consider your career."

The National Education Association offers numerous examples of an ethic focused primarily on consequences:

The National Education Association opposes—

• alcohol and tobacco *dependency*

• appropriate educational experiences to educate students about the *serious consequences* of participating in any aspect of the illegal drug trade

• improved education programs about the *serious effects* of participating in any aspect of the illegal drug trade

• *denying federal financial aid* to college students who have been convicted of misdemeanor, nonviolent drug offenses (emphasis mine) (NEA, 2009)

One easily can see that NEA is concerned primarily with *dependency* on alcohol and tobacco and not on the use of either. Moreover NEA's interest rests in educating participants in illegal drug trade about the *serious consequences and effects* of participation, not the participation itself.

Evaluating one's thinking

With this in mind we can more easily understand precisely why "think before you drink" remains inadequate as a moral guide. First, no one can predict with certainty what the consequences of any act will bring. Also, if moral acts are based on good results that follow from the act, what happens when the projected results are not so good? For example if a young adult jumped into a lake to save a drowning child but the child drowned after all, one would have to judge, based on results, that the act of jumping in the lake was not a moral good for the simple reason no moral good came from it.

Second, how does the moral guide that focuses on consequences deal with people who beat the system? Some people drink and drive but never have had an accident or even have been stopped by the police. Many people who abuse drugs live in mansions and drive fine cars. Some people cheat on tests but go on to be professors in universities. In a world whose moral construct centers around good results, one could conclude that drunken driving, abusing drugs, and cheating on tests are at best amoral and at worst arbitrarily immoral. In the end, however, we seemingly cannot build a moral guide simply on our predictions of the outcome. Thus "think before you drink" is simply one notch morally better than having no moral at all.

Third, expecting teen-agers and young adults to "think" before they consume intoxicating substances is both presumptuous and naïve. The chemical composition for ethyl alcohol, otherwise known as alcohol, is C_2H_5OH (*Encyclopedia of Alcohol*, 2009). The formula indicates composure of two carbons, one oxygen, and six atoms of hydrogen. Ethanol is colorless liquid, highly flammable, and dangerously addictive. Aside from being in beer, wines, and other alcoholic beverages, ethanol is used in fuels, disinfectants, and cleaners. Imagine it: a person craving social stimulation from the additives in liquid plumbing supplies!

Ethanol works under stealth on the central nervous system. It subtly adds danger as it chips away at one's natural inhibitions. It relaxes moral restraints and gives a false sense of courage to act in ways one would not act otherwise. To envision teen-agers and young adults possessing sufficient mental and emotional weaponry to resist such a secret invader is to envision the absurd.

In addition asking one to practice "thinking before the drinking" completely ignores the real purpose for drinking in the first place. People do not drink alcoholic beverages because they're thirsty. People drink alcoholic beverages for the buzz—the sheer pleasure and delight of experiencing the drug itself.

Conclusion

Thus, suggesting one "think" before popping open a beer can is like suggesting one "think" before attending a rock concert, a football game, a pizza party, or any other event, the purpose of which is to offer the participants a certain amount of pleasure. If grown, mature, and successful adults cannot resist the subtle power of intoxicating substances and the pleasure those substances offer, how do we expect the youngest, and in many ways, the weakest in our society to resist? "Think before you drink" is a dead ethic. In the end it adds to the problem of consuming intoxicating substances for pleasurable purposes. It certainly does not solve the problem.

Part 2

Chapter 7

"Drink but Don't Get Drunk"

With *hedonism*—the view that virtually deifies pleasure as the highest achievement, the highest moral value—we began our journey in examining five views on consuming intoxicating substances. We then moved across state and traveled to a sister city, where the chief goal was to suggest to those who consume intoxicating substances that they "think" first. Unfortunately, when this goal was weighed in the balance of common sense, it wound up woefully wanting—a dead ethic, just as dead as its sister ethic before.

We're now on the road again. For the first time we pass a major boundary and travel across the state line, if you will, into new moral territory. In other words, a definitive switch takes place at this juncture. Whereas before we were dealing with secularly-driven moral forms—hedonism and utilitarianism—we now cross the line to moral forms influenced primarily by a decidedly Christian worldview. Put simply, Christian morals are now considered.

Ground rules and moral principles

As we cross the border into this new moral territory we've described as being distinctively influenced by the Christian worldview, we're obligated to introduce some ground rules to better understand the terrain we're in. Several matters present themselves.

First, unlike our first two moral positions, the Christian moral position is a revealed moral position. That is, Christian ethics is rooted in God's revelation about righteousness. Technically, this position is dubbed in ethical studies as *divine command theory*. Whatever the case, the premise on which we build our understanding of the good, the right, and the just is the Self-revelation of God Himself. Furthermore a Christian moral position is, as we stated earlier, non-negotiably wed to biblical revelation as His Self-revelation, the inspired hub of every moral position we embrace.

We do not insist on equal clarity from Scripture about every conceivable moral issue we encounter. *Thou shalt not commit adultery* translates almost flawlessly from ancient Hebrew culture to our own contemporary culture. That is, adultery now is equitable to adultery then. On the other hand, *When thou buildest a new house, then thou shalt make a battlement for thy roof, that thou bring not blood upon thine house, if any man fall from thence* (Deut. 22:8) is not, without much consideration, properly translatable and applicable to modern society. Particularly contemporary medical science and quantum leaps in medical technology pose innumerable new challenges for Christian moral thinkers (Davis, 1985). Even so, we remain confident even if the Bible—God's Revealed Word—does not *directly* speak to all moral issues, nevertheless it *indirectly* speaks to every conceivable moral decision we may encounter.

When we are faced with moral questions about which the Bible does not directly address, while it may at times be challenging, the Christian is not left to himself or herself to "make do" alone. With the assistance of proper hermeneutical practices in interpreting the Word of God and general moral principles harvested from such careful research, sound moral decisions may confidently be reached—decisions that speak authoritatively to every area of life. Anything less remains absolutely inadequate as a Christian alternative (Feinberg & Feinberg, 1993).

Hence while we may *discover* moral principles as we face moral situations that the Bible does not specifically or directly address, we most certainly cannot *create* moral principles from those situations. Once again Christian ethics is *revealed* ethics. Through careful study of biblical revelation we allow the general moral principle(s) we glean to guide our moral decision-making in areas not directly addressed by Scripture (Geisler & Feinberg, 1980).

*Second, unlike our first two moral positions, which in no sense claimed any high moral ground, Christian ethics necessarily is **absolutist** in nature.* By absolutist is meant an immobile moral—a fixed moral anchor concerning which, no matter the time, the place, the era, the culture, the people, the circumstances, or any other changeable circumstance, the moral action called for transcends such and is confidently considered the good, the right, and the just. *In short, the Christian worldview requires moral absolutes.*

Erwin Lutzer, in his insightful little volume, *The Necessity of Ethical Absolutes*, examines one by one four popular ethical systems—Cultural Relativism, Situation Ethics, Behaviorism, Emotive Ethics—and ably demonstrates the impossibility of building a consistent moral position apart from dependence on moral absolutes (Lutzer, 1981). Thus a moral position based on Christian premises substantially undermines those ethical systems absent of such foundation and shows them fundamentally incoherent. Christian morality begins with the greatest Absolute of all: God Almighty Himself. Francis Schaeffer put it like this: "It is not that there's a moral absolute behind God that binds man and God, because that which is farthest back is always finally God. Rather, it is God Himself and his character who is the moral absolute of the universe" (Schaeffer, 1982).

*Third, a decidedly Christian ethic is **deontological** in nature. Deontological* is another one of those $50 terms making plain denim into designer jeans. So what does it mean? Think of *deontological* as having to do with one's moral *duty* or *obligation* to do the right thing. For example one's moral duty is to speak truth and not falsehood. If a person is married, moral duty means to remain faithful to one's spouse. If one is a parent, moral duty requires providing a home for the children. Thus, even though *deontological* sounds highly complicated and is used only in textbooks and theory, when the term is teased out in everyday life, it makes a lot more sense. Just think of it as identifiable moral rules and principles by which to live.

Additionally, note a significant contrast from another term we used earlier. Recall we spoke of "teleological" ethics. *Teleological* concerns itself with consequences, outcomes, or results to determine whether an action is a moral one. Suppose for example we consider the astronomical number of unwed mothers in our society as completely unacceptable (and, of course it is!) and therefore needing to be addressed. Suppose further we reason the quickest, easiest, most economical, and most effective means by which to lower the number of unwed mothers to a perfectly acceptable level is to make abortion exceptionally easy, convenient, and free and to offer such services to all minors including full protective privacy from any parental input. Thus, because the acceptable level of unwed mothers, which is the moral good sought, would best be attainable through easy abortion, easy abortion becomes a moral act. Hopefully, the contrast is clear: *a deontological moral position focuses primarily upon behaving in the right way quite apart from the behavior's result.*

Do not misunderstand: certainly I'm not saying that we don't consider results at all when we speak of moral absolutes. Instead what we are considering is that *outcomes do not determine one's action; principle does.* As another example a pastor may consider the *outcome* of confronting unruly church members who happen to be the largest group of contributors to the church budget and what may happen as a result if the group is confronted. Nevertheless, if scriptural principle demands confrontation take place, the pastor possesses no liberty to cancel out the principle because the results may be regretful. He acts on *principled rule* and not *projected results*.

As important as the group may be to the health of the church's budget, a *deontological* moral decision stands on the principle of Scripture that instructs confrontation, not the reasoned result—likely or not—that projects that if the group is confronted, members may cease giving to the budget. While making distinctions such as these may be taxing on our minds at times, our grasping some of them is crucial to fully understand what's at stake in abandoning the biblical ethic of abstinence.

Do moral guides collide?

One final note before we move further. Sometimes moral absolutes *collide* with each other. One illustration is the well-worn but marvelous story of the Dutch Christian, Corrie ten Boom, and her heroic actions in hiding Jewish refugees in a secret room from Hitler's Third Reich thugs and lying to the soldiers when they asked her about it. She *did not tell them the truth*. Yet *she saved Jewish people's lives* from concentration death camps. Was she immoral to lie? Or, was she righteous to save lives? Christian thinkers, especially those committed to biblical revelation, wrestle with these issues.

Ethicist Joseph Fletcher mistakenly built an entire ethical theory called "situational ethics" on moral dilemmas such as ten Boom faced. These are captured by his colorful moral cliche, "there are times when a man has to push his principles aside and do the right thing" (Fletcher, 1966). Fletcher's flawed answer was to discard biblical revelation altogether. More careful Christians such as John Murray represents see these moral dilemmas an inevitable result of a sinful world. Thus sometimes we're faced with choosing between two moral evils, the lesser evil of which is the path to take (Murray, 1957). Most of us have heard or even said about a decision, "I chose the lesser of two evils." In this particular case, ten Boom's lying was wrong; however, turning the Jews over to the Gestapo would have been much more tragic.

Still others like Norman Geisler, John and Paul Feinberg, and W. D. Ross argue for what can be called the greater of two goods. In this particular case ten Boom would have acted morally good in telling the truth. Truth-telling is a moral good. But saving innocent human life, when trapped in a moral dilemma, takes moral precedence over telling the truth to human butchers. Hence, deciding the lesser of two evils is not applicable; instead the greater of two goods is at stake. As Geisler perceptively asks, "when lying and lives are weighed, are not lives more important?"

The reason I bring this up is because many times Christians do not understand the nature of moral absolutes. Consequently moral absolutism is confused with moral legalism. The two definitively are not the same. Moral absolutes are required in Christian ethics and remain the biblical expression of authentic faith in Jesus Christ. We are saved by faith in Jesus Christ alone, with absolutely nothing to add to the justification before God such faith brings. Yet obeying scriptural norms does not add nor earn grace from God. Neither does such obedience establish our relationship with God.

According to Scripture moral legalism seeks God's favor— God's grace by virtue of the action performed. For example Luke writes of the apostolic conference, *And certain men which came down from Judaea taught the brethren, and said, Except ye be circumcised after the manner of Moses, ye cannot be saved . . . saying, That it was needful to circumcise them, and to command them to keep the law of Moses . . . Forasmuch as we have heard, that certain which went out from us have troubled you with words, subverting your souls, saying, Ye must be circumcised, and keep the law: to whom we gave no such commandment* (Acts 15:1, 5, 24). Clearly the focus of these legalistic Judaizers is to add to the sufficiency and finality of Christ's redemptive death and resurrection. They are suggesting one cannot be saved apart from keeping laws, especially as this relates to circumcision. Hence, moral legalism is not about acting morally but about earning grace.

The Apostle Paul later squares off with the same Jewish sect we find in Acts 15 whom he slices and dices for bewitching the Galatian believers. Marveling because they are *so soon removed* from the simplicity of the gospel of grace he preaches, apparently turning to *another gospel*, Paul bluntly asks them: *O foolish Galatians, who hath bewitched you . . . This only would I learn of you, Received ye the Spirit by the works of the law, or by the hearing of faith? Are ye so foolish? having begun in the Spirit, are ye now made perfect by the flesh?* (Gal. 1:6; 3:1-3).

The meaning appears obvious. In the text these false teachers attempt to earn God's favor through keeping the law. The Apostle Paul sabotages such efforts to undermine the redemptive power of the cross.

As our faith-life is teased out day-to-day—what we call *sanctification*—the Lordship of Jesus Christ guides us in holiness and righteousness before God, as revealed both *directly* and *indirectly* in biblical revelation. Our holiness as disciples of Jesus expresses itself through the ethical norms we call *moral absolutes*. In other words to insist on moral absolutes is not moral legalism; it is Christian discipleship.

No Christian in modern times has pleaded more passionately for the necessity of moral absolutes than did Francis Schaeffer, who argues a fundamental shift in our value system took place between the years 1913 to 1940 in the American culture (Schaeffer, 1982). During that time, Schaeffer contends, we lost the idea that moral absolutes are necessary. One way this loss of absolutes translates is in the idea of "antithesis." This sounds complicated, but the way Schaeffer means it is very simple. If A is true, the opposite of A is false. Or, speaking more applicably for our purposes, if A is right, then the opposite of A is wrong. Again, how many times have you heard one say, "that's right for you, but it's not right for me"?

And, lest one think that such is not an overwhelming problem not only in our culture but also in evangelical Christianity, the latest research suggests otherwise: "One-third of all adults (34 percent) believe that moral truth is absolute and unaffected by the circumstances. Slightly less than half of the born-again adults (46 percent) believe in absolute moral truth" (Research, 2009). One out of three adults denying moral absolutes clearly shows why our culture continues to be obsessed with fulfilling selfish, hedonistic desires. What's more frightening is that not even half of all "born-again adults" believe in moral absolutes!

If this is so, it may explain precisely why an undeniable flirtation with the pursuit of pleasure—that is, hedonism—continues to exist. The way I see it, evidence of this could be the open, public advocacy for the recreational consumption of alcoholic beverages. Additionally, such a dismal picture depicting the severe absence of moral absolutes among evangelical Christians goes a long way in understanding why those of us who embrace moral absolutes are confused with embracing moral legalism.

Therefore, applying moral legalism to the moderate consumption of intoxicating substances for recreational purposes is not only wrong-headed, it is ill-informed and betrays a basic confusion between moral absolutism and moral legalism. The former is necessary not only to Christian duty but also Christian doctrine. On the other hand moral legalism remains an ugly, sub-Christian moral add-on to biblical faith.

"Drink but don't get drunk"

With the above introduction in mind, let's look at what has become perhaps the default view of the Christian church about the recreational consumption of intoxicating beverages—**moderation**. The mantra espoused is very clear, very memorable: *The Bible condemns the abuse of intoxicating drink, not the* *use of intoxicating drink*. The clear distinction is between "use" and "abuse." The mere consuming or "using" of intoxicating beverage holds absolutely no moral culpability. In fact, as moderationists build their moral case for consuming alcoholic substances even for recreational purposes, they inevitably begin by quoting biblical references that suggest wine is part and parcel of God's good creation about which we should be thankful:

*Therefore God give thee of the dew of heaven, and the fatness of the earth, and **plenty of corn and wine** (Gen. 27:28, emphasis added here and following).*

*He causeth the grass to grow for the cattle, and herb for the service of man: that he may bring forth food out of the earth; And **wine that maketh glad the heart of man**, and oil to make his face to shine, and bread which strengtheneth man's heart (Ps. 104:14-15).*

*Go thy way, eat thy bread with joy, and **drink thy wine with a merry heart**; for God now accepteth thy works (Eccl. 9:7).*

*Ho, every one that thirsteth, come ye to the waters, and he that hath no money; come ye, buy, and eat; yea, come, **buy wine and milk without money and without price** (Isa. 55:1).*

*Even all the Jews returned out of all places whither they were driven, and came to the land of Judah, to Gedaliah, unto Mizpah, and **gathered wine and summer fruits very much** (Jer. 40:12).*

*Behold, the days come, saith the Lord, that the plowman shall overtake the reaper, and the treader of grapes him that soweth seed; and the mountains shall drop **sweet wine**, and all the hills shall melt (Amos 9:13).*

The verses above represent only a small sampling of biblical passages that refer to positive images the Bible offers toward *wine*. While we intend to deal later on a more comprehensive level with verses such as these, four matters need immediate attention.

Weighing moderation in the balance of the Bible and common sense

First, rehearsing passages from the Bible that offer *positive* support for a particular moral position—*in this case, wine is to be enjoyed in moderation*—without also fairly dealing with those passages that appear to negate the position one is advocating is both unacceptable and inadequate in forging a moral construct—especially a moral position in which its foundation is the Word of God. The truth is, as we shall see later, many passages of Scripture offer *negative* support for consuming wine.

Second, the unproven premise on which moderation is constructed is that whenever the Bible speaks of *wine*, it speaks of only one particular type of *wine*; *that is, wine which is fermented and therefore intoxicating.* We intend to show this premise to be both unproven and unlikely. Consequently, if we are correct, the entire moral construct of moderately consuming alcoholic beverages for recreational purposes collapses. If God commends some wines (non-intoxicating) but condemns others (intoxicating), no moral case can be made from Scripture for the recreational use of intoxicating beverages today. Even more, if no moral case can be made for intoxicating beverages, we possess full moral authority to make a solid case against the recreational use of any and all intoxicating substances regardless of whether it is consumed in beverages, swallowed as capsules, or directly injected. Obviously, the medicinal usage of drugs is not in view. The Bible makes this clear (cp. [compare passage] 1 Tim. 5:23; more on this passage follows).

Third, even granting the premise on which moderationists build their moral case in approving the recreational use of intoxicating drink—*namely, when Scripture speaks of wine, it is always fermented wine*—does not relieve them of the hermeneutical tension in applying their moral premise today. For even if all wines mentioned in the Bible were fermented, we are incorrect in assuming that the wine then is remotely related to alcoholic beverages now. New Testament professor Robert Stein wrote, "Drinking wine unmixed . . . was looked upon as a 'scythian' or barbarian custom" (Stein, 1975). Why? According to Stein in biblical times the wine that was commonly used was diluted with water at the normal ratio of three parts water to one part wine. This means modern alcoholic beverages frequently possess alcoholic content "three to ten times greater" than wines of antiquity. Accordingly "one would have to drink over twenty-two glasses . . . to consume the amount of alcohol that is in two martinis" !

Not that becoming intoxicated from drinking the wine in biblical times was impossible. Indeed the record is clear pertaining to the problem of drunkenness. The first mention of wine in the Bible is connected with Noah's drunken stupor (Gen. 9:20-24). Instead Stein concludes, "one's drinking would probably affect the bladder long before it affected the mind."

Thus we can see that if moderationists desire to directly translate for today their moral principle concerning the acceptable consumption of intoxicating wine as found in Scripture, at minimum they would need to dilute each serving of today's wines with such a substantial amount of ordinary tap water that it would render the wine both obnoxious to the taste and practically nil as to effect. What moderationist argues for such a position? I can answer in one word—*none*.

Moreover, moderationists commit what 19th-century renowned biblical scholar Frederic Lees called "the same error of interpretation that so long perverted and confused the Slavery question." What error was that? It was the error of applying "ancient words, and ancient ideas expressed by them, to modern things, modern relations, and modern practices, which, though covered by the same general language, had undergone a change so great, as to amount to almost a radical difference" (Lees, Burns, & Lewis, 1870). For example, consider the wide distance between the Abrahamic relation of chieftain and servant followers, toward which the commercial ideas of trafficking human souls were almost wholly unknown, and the vile, merciless, human-degrading slavery of modern times. The error of slavery-advocates was clear: *they wrongly read their twisted ideas back into the sacred text to justify their immoral exploitation in buying and selling the souls of men and women for the best market price.*

Similarly Lees argued that those who defended the moderate consumption of intoxicating beverages erred in his day when they applied the simple language of Scripture as it was often used of harmless substances—in many instances, the pure, freshly-squeezed juice of the grape—to the vile and noxious compounds which, in modern times, pass under similar names. Distilled intoxicants, artificially fortified as they were with an extra-added amount of intoxicating "kick", and the global liquor industry that predictably depended on recruiting younger and younger drinkers to remain economically viable, could hardly be morally equitable to the life-giving **viticulture** of ancient Palestine that depended chiefly on the grape harvest itself for survival. Lees concludes about his day, "Anti-temperance critics are fond of charging the zealous temperance advocate with perversions of Scripture and strained interpretations. This is doubtless true in some cases, *but the fault is far more apt to be on the other side*" (Lees, Burns, & Lewis, 1870).

Even in our day the industry produces more and more products specifically to attract younger consumers. The notorious "wine coolers" and "alcopops," the latter of which arrives on the market in rich, neon colors and flavored with titillating fruit juices, are favorites among teen-agers. Nonetheless, the intoxicating content nicely covered over by the fruity flavors is competitive with other beers and malt liquors.

The usual argument from moderationists has been that the Bible, in spite of the warnings by moral principle and biblical example against drunkenness, not only does not prohibit the drinking of wine but also even encourages it. However, if we stopped and went no further with our investigation, enough has been established thus far to firmly question the moderationist's assertion indicating consuming intoxicating beverages is both morally acceptable and socially approved for the Christian community.

Fourth, if moderationists are correct about their premise that when Scripture speaks of wine, it is always intoxicating wine—including the moral trajectory they deduce, namely, the Bible condemns the *abuse* of intoxicating wine, not the *use* of intoxicating wine—one must wonder how moderationists can consistently argue for the moral acceptability of recreationally consuming intoxicating substances in beverage drinks but reject as morally acceptable the recreational use of intoxicating substances consumed in non-beverage ways.

For example, since, for the moderationist, the intoxicating substance in wine is morally acceptable and socially approved —in moderate amounts, of course—would the recreational smoking of marijuana, in moderate amounts, not also be morally acceptable and socially approved? And even though cocaine is highly toxic to the central nervous system, theoretically at least small enough amounts possibly could be consumed so as to fit the criteria "moderation." If so, what moral reservation does the moderationist raise against recreational cocaine use, since the only intoxicant about which we know in Scripture has been happily validated on the moderationist's own terms? Countless other intoxicating substances could be mentioned but would only serve redundancy.

The fact is, given the moderationist's moral premises, he or she nails firmly in place the moral construct that inevitably lacks the stability to resist the perpetual theoretical winds howling for the legalization of all intoxicating substances. Frankly, if moderation is the moral rule of thumb, **Libertinism** can break out the champagne buckets. They've just found a new partner that may lead them to their stated goal—*drug legalization*.

84

Some moderationists attempt to avoid the devastating impact that considering other drugs into their moral framework delivers to their position by arguing that drugs such as marijuana and cocaine are illegal and therefore immoral. Drawing from Scripture's validation of societal law, advocates for moderation in consuming intoxicating beverages reason that since government is ordained by God, we should consider breaking such law immoral (cp. Rom. 13:1-6). While we surely have no objection to giving Caesar precisely what Caesar is due (Mt. 22:21a), we dare not be less concerned in giving to God precisely what God is due (Mt. 22:21b). Somewhere we're told, are we not, we ought to obey God's law rather than human law (Acts 5:29)? In effect, God's law outranks human law by a gazillion Georgia miles!

More troubling is the entirely inadequate moral equation of things *illegal* with things *immoral*. If this is so, is not the contrary true? That is, *legal* things are *moral* things. How such a moral construct fits evangelicals' almost universal abhorrence of abortion on demand, as right as such moral abhorrence may be, is hardly understandable. For if the legal is also the moral, then legal abortion is also moral abortion.

The fact is, government's authority—including moral authority—is to be honored and respected. However, government's authority is, at best, merely relative. In other words, as long as government's authority does not conflict with our higher authority, we are to honor governmental authority. Nonetheless biblical Christians rightly take moral marching orders from a higher, Absolute Authority, Who's spoken His moral principles in the Word of God. Consequently, biblical Christians forge moral principles first from Scripture. Only afterward are legal principles properly considered.

Therefore, if we are correct, we may sum up and rightly draw this conclusion about the "drink but don't get drunk" position: if the case can be made that consuming moderate amounts of intoxicating substances in beverage drinks for recreational use is morally and biblically acceptable, we can presume that the case for consuming moderate amounts of intoxicating substances in non-beverage means for recreational use also is morally and biblically acceptable. The moderationist cannot have it both ways. Either intoxicating substances in moderate amounts are morally acceptable in both wine and non-wine means or else intoxicating substances in moderate amounts are morally acceptable in neither.

Conclusion

For the church to possess a policy that favors the recreational consumption of alcohol appears strange, to say the least. Even more problematic, however, is the passive approach that many evangelical denominations possess toward intoxicating drink. As we learned in chapter two, evangelicals were all but unanimous in their support of total abstinence from intoxicating beverages, which led up to legalized Prohibition. One laments not only their biblical about-face concerning intoxicants but also the moral message received by the youngest in our society.

The church forfeited the high moral ground by conceding the behavior of drink is intrinsically amoral in nature. For moderationists, imbibing intoxicating drink fits into the category of choosing vanilla over chocolate—so long as one does not get drunk. The *use* of drink does not involve ungodliness; rather the *abuse* of drink is the moral evil, according to the prophets of moderation. One simply should have stopped shy of being drunk. Nevertheless, to position into the category of *adiaphora* a highly addictive and decidedly dangerous drug like ethanol alcohol, which arguably is instrumental in more destruction, both domestic and societal, than is any other single element, can only be described as morally delusional.

Some moderationists such as Ken Gentry actually believe the Bible teaches that we should be thankful to God for the buzz we receive from alcohol. He writes, "In fact, a moderate 'gladdening of the heart' [Gentry means alcoholic effects] is not forbidden according to [the] Scriptures" (Gentry, 2001). One Southern Baptist pastor in Montgomery, AL, appears to wholeheartedly agree. On a Baptist blog he wrote virtually the very same in an exchange we had about Psalm 104:14-15. Concerning God's creation of intoxicating wine, the pastor logged these shocking words: "How can wine gladden the heart of man if it has no effect on him? It seems like this would be referring to something in the wine that made people happy. Could it be alcohol? And, it is saying that God made it as though it is a good thing. *Yes, I do believe that alcohol was present here to gladden the heart of men. The wine had an effect on the person to gladden his heart and that was not seen as a bad thing in and of itself.*" So God allegedly created the buzz for which we could be "made happy."

What does all of this mean for the younger generation in the church? Tragically it means this: when a young man or woman is instructed by the church that consuming intoxicating beverages is both morally acceptable and socially approved, and thus he or she may confidently consume alcohol with full biblical authority quite apart from moral remorse or guilt—just so long as he or she does not become drunk—*the stripped-down moral principle stands naked for all to see: consuming intoxicants is perfectly biblical and therefore acceptably moral. Just be careful how much you consume.*

As another young Southern Baptist pastor put it, "The biblical point doesn't change. It's abuse that is the problem, not the alcohol content. You can sip whiskey, mix it with cola, or whatever. *As long as you don't get drunk and drink for the glory of God, you are cool, biblically speaking.*" Drinking for the glory of God? You'll be *cool, biblically speaking*? Not likely, I'm afraid. Even mature adults are highly vulnerable to alcohol's addiction. Do we then expect young people to strangely resist its magnetic attraction?

Indeed to tell a young person to go ahead and drink but don't get drunk is like telling a fox, after you've locked him in the henhouse, he can touch the chickens but cannot taste the chickens. If asking precisely why young people drink in the first place ever occurred to those who advocate drinking without drunkenness, one would not know it.

Interestingly while drunkenness is rightly seen as condemned in Scripture, this position offers no substantial difference from the "*Think Before You Drink*" view. That is, fundamentally the two are morally equivalent. The difference is in what constitutes *responsible* or *abusive* drinking. Neither position associates drinking itself with illicit behavior.

In conclusion the view that says "drink but don't get drunk" suspiciously looks as if it is based largely on results. The *act* of drinking clearly is not what remains in question for moderationists. Rather what remains in question is the *outcome* of drinking—or rather, too much drinking—which is drunkenness. Hence the concern is with the consequence, outcome, and result. In short, the moderationist message shrinks to little more than an innocuous moral message from a secular culture without Christ.

Nor is it premature, even in this stage of our argument's development, to advance an incitable observation others in an earlier era constructed about the moderationist view of consuming intoxicating beverages. Focusing on the *outcome* of drinking intoxicating beverages rather than the *act* of drinking itself firmly places the moderationist view in moral jeopardy, as we have seen, because, at least at that juncture, moderation looks much more like secular culture's view of intoxicating substances than it does a Christian moral view of intoxicating substances.

Perhaps a more potent protest, if possible, against moderationists' view of recreationally consuming intoxicating beverages is this: moderation decidedly connects much more with the ethics of ancient Greece—that is, the "golden mean", with

Aristotle still standing as its legendary champion—than it does with the ethics of Jesus and the Apostles.

J. Maurice Trimmer writes: "Moderation in drinking is called 'temperance.' That is an Aristotelian but not a Christian virtue. Aristotle based his ethical teaching on the 'golden mean.' Thus he held that thrift is the mean between miserliness and prodigality, courtesy the mean between flattery and contempt, courage the mean between boasting and servility. He sought to elevate 'moderation in all things' into a moral principle that would be a safe guide to conduct in all circumstances. But the Hebrew-Christian view is different. Adultery is wrong, whether committed 'reasonably and with restraint' or otherwise . . . It is total abstinence that is demanded, and there are sound reasons for insisting that total abstinence is the only practice that fulfills the requirements of Christian morality with reference to intoxicating beverages" (Trimmer, 1946). For this reason and others Trimmer rightly brands moderately consuming intoxicating beverages as an immoral *menace* to both social community and societal health.

Chapter 8

"Don't Wine Up; Wise Up"

"Knowledge is a process of piling up facts; wisdom lies in their simplification," wrote one author. What's both captured and contrasted in this winsome proverb from today is the dual nature of the good, the right, and the just. On the one hand truth—including moral truth—can be excruciatingly complex, as in "piling up facts." On the other hand, however, truth—again including moral truth—can be strikingly simple, as in wisdom's "simplification." In many ways wisdom may be described as truth that possesses a self-evident feel about it, almost as if wisdom needs no proof; wisdom just is. Never mind whether one is scholar or illiterate. Wisdom can be perceived by all.

The comedian George Burns once indicated "it's too bad all the people who really know how to run the country are busy driving taxi cabs and cutting hair." This was a humorous way of saying even in sophisticated matters such as running the globe's largest economy, true wisdom possesses a profound, self-evident simplicity about it. The capacity to perceive wisdom is a God-given capacity bestowed on us—every human being—as we're made in the image of God. Even the most illiterate among us intuitively knows the wrongness of using hot pokers to torture crying babies. Thus, moral wisdom possesses, in some sense, a self-evident simplicity knowable by the masses of humanity.

The Bible on wisdom

Nor is this all, for the Bible places an inestimable value on wisdom. Job tells us wisdom is eternal, for wisdom is found deeply seated in the Almighty Himself: *Behold, God is mighty, and despiseth not any: he is mighty in strength and wisdom* (36:5). Through wisdom God creates the cosmos and places in position human rulers on the earth (Ps. 104:24; 105:22; 136:5).

As we speak wisdom, we speak righteousness (Ps. 37:30). Therefore, wisdom must be both prayed for and applied (Ps. 51:6; 90:12). In fact for the Christian, pursuing wisdom siphons from our inner tank every last drop of motivation until bone dry. By far the wisest of his era, good King Solomon personifies wisdom's chase. He likens the pursuit to a man in passionate quest of a virgin bride. He puts it like this:

Get wisdom, get understanding: forget it not; neither decline from the words of my mouth. Forsake her not, and she shall preserve thee: love her, and she shall keep thee. Wisdom is the principal thing; therefore get wisdom: and with all thy getting get understanding. Exalt her, and she shall promote thee: she shall bring thee to honour, when thou dost embrace her. She shall give to thine head an ornament of grace: a crown of glory shall she deliver to thee (Prov. 4:5-9).

The wisdom view: does it have weaknesses?

As we've seen above, wisdom's value in constructing a moral view generally cannot be overestimated. However, more applicable to our subject, neither is wisdom's value in properly judging the rightness or wrongness of recreationally consuming intoxicating substances taken for granted. Hence, as we examine this view, may the reader keep in mind the profound respect I possess for this premise.

And, since I will offer some mild criticism—weaknesses that I believe nudge us to embrace more than this view—in no uncertain terms should one suppose that I reject the wisdom view. To the contrary I fully embrace the wisdom view and surely shelter no intentions to eliminate it. Nonetheless, what I do insist on is both embracing the wisdom view and building on it—indeed going beyond it to what I argue reflects a more comprehensive biblical understanding (more in the next chapter).

With such an introduction in mind, we're now in a position to speak plainly about what I call the *wisdom view* on the consumption of intoxicating substances. This position is the mainstay of those who still deny that consuming intoxicants for recreational use is morally acceptable even in so-called "moderate" amounts. It appeals to evangelicals at large because it bases its case on biblical premises (as noted above) and concludes abstinence is the best, wisest choice

More than likely, it is held by most Southern Baptists—or at least, a significantly large portion—and has been argued effectively by Drs. Richard Land and Barrett Duke *et al*. I call this the "wisdom view" because its primary moral trajectory, I believe, is viewing drinking as an <u>unwise</u> practice: *Wine is a mocker, strong drink is raging: and whosoever is deceived thereby is not wise* (Prov. 20:1). Some wisdom advocates such as Land and Duke possess a more pliable moral construct and progressively move wisdom *toward* absolutism, as we'll see in a moment.

Also this premise makes much of the admonition of the Apostle Paul who speaks of drinking as potentially harmful to others: *It is good neither to eat flesh, nor to drink wine, nor any thing whereby thy brother stumbleth, or is offended, or is made weak* (Rom. 14:21). Moreover drinking even in moderate amounts risks one's Christian testimony, a further indication that moderation lacks wisdom.

Of course this by no means suggests that the case made for abstinence by advocates of wisdom contains no more sophistication than the moral sketch I've briefly outlined above. To the contrary Land and Duke construct one of the best cases in print for the wisdom view, which by the way, is the major reason I chose their paper to engage.

Nevertheless the wisdom view clearly focuses more on whether one is *wise* to drink than on whether one is *moral* to drink. No better summary illustrates such than Land and Duke's own words as they conclude about Paul's instruction about church leaders: "To be sure, *none of these passages require abstinence. Their concern is related to over-indulgence.* It would also appear that Paul is speaking about regular practice. The people about whom Paul is speaking are those whose lives are characterized by *excessive* use of alcohol. According to Paul, church leaders were not to *habitually drink alcohol in excess.* If they did, they were *disqualified* from leadership" (emphasis added).

If I have not misread the authors' intention, the implication is clear. Namely, Paul's instruction addresses not consuming intoxicating substances *per se.* Instead he addresses excessive use, over-indulgence, and habitually drinking alcohol to excess. One wonders, given these terms of the Apostle Paul's meaning, how the entire moral structure, in the end, is significantly different from those who advocate moderation. After all, if consuming intoxicants by the church calls for moral guidance from apostolic authority, and Paul's moral concern remains on "over-indulgence" and "excessive use of alcohol," and thus concluding, as do Land and Duke "none of these passages require abstinence", I'm under the impression that those who embrace the moderate consumption of intoxicants would happily say, "That's what we've been saying all along!"

In fairness Land and Duke's wisdom view contains absolutist yearnings. For example in the paragraph following the citation above, the authors write: "This should not be interpreted to mean, however, that these passages *permit church leaders to drink alcoholic beverages . . .* Even *less plausible* are arguments from these passages in *support of the recreational/social use of alcohol today*" (emphasis added). They later add, "there appears to be a clear movement in Scripture toward a rejection of alcohol use." For them the moderate drinker should find no comfort in the passages assembled to sanction his or her recreational use of alcohol. The moral trajectory of Scripture clearly thrusts us toward an abstinence position.

Without reservation we agree with Land and Duke's conclusion. Our difference with them is exactly how we arrive at our mutual destination. In other words we agree with them about abstinence, but we question the strength of their premises to sustain it. For example even though they offer a lengthy discussion on why the passages they assemble do not "permit church leaders to drink", I'm far from persuaded that their prior interpretative conclusion is overturned: "*none of these passages require abstinence.* Their concern is related to *overindulgence . . .* by *excessive* use of alcohol." Also, if a "clear movement in Scripture toward a rejection of alcohol use" exists, one must wonder—when we get to the instructions Paul gives for church leaders at the tail-end of biblical revelation—why Land and Duke could not conclude other than "*none* of these passages *require* abstinence."

The authors undoubtedly have thought their position through. We highly respect their work. Moreover, we once again say we fully agree with their conclusion—*abstinence*. Yet the lack of clear answers to the questions above only nudges us further to construct a case for abstinence on what we believe is a stronger platform.

Conclusion

The proponents of the wisdom view offer <u>powerful reasons</u> and, so far as they go, <u>compelling reasons</u> for not consuming intoxicating drinks. The difficulties are created by what many wisdom advocates concede to those who argue for moderation. Frankly, as we've noted above, we think far too much concession is illegitimately granted them toward propping up their hopeless moderation ethic.

In many respects moderationists agree with the wisdom view when it asserts drinking given any number of circumstances may not be wise. For example, for alcoholics or anyone, for that matter, who cannot control his or her consumption to drink is unwise. Pregnant women are unwise to consume alcohol—indeed even the smallest amount of intoxicating drink—while carrying their child. For pastors to consume alcohol, since it could tarnish their reputations among some people, also is unwise. Nonetheless moderationists are quick to point out that while drinking for these reasons and more may be unwise, not all non-medicinal consumption of alcohol necessarily must be viewed as unwise.

Consequently if this type of consumption is not unwise in all respects, moderationists rightly ask, how can a blanket prohibition against the reasonable, responsible consumption of alcohol be biblically defended? As Land and Duke conceded above, the Apostle Paul is concerned with *excessive* drink, not drink in itself. Even more, apparently for them, disqualification from church leadership results *only if the church leaders habitually drank alcohol in excess.* Therefore if the Bible does not condemn the *use* of alcohol *per se* but only its *unwise* use—what they call *excess*—on what moral basis can the church make general admonitions for abstinence from recreational consumption of intoxicating beverages?

Again, if I am correct, is the conclusion not inevitable? The wisdom view, as great as it is and as popular as it remains, appears to lack the impetus to successfully argue for abstinence in moral absolutist terms—*the moral absolutes of which stand as the hub of Christian ethics*—but can only *encourage* abstinence because it is a wise decision. But then again who is against encouraging abstinence, the moderationists quickly inquire? They certainly would not plead guilty to such. In fact many moderationists consistently practice abstinence.

Given such a compelling rebuttal by moderationists, wisdom-view advocates are forced to fall back on the "bad example" strategy from which they draw Roman 14:21. Granted. But what about the guy who does a Bible study in his home and enjoys wine with a group of believers, none of whom is in jeopardy of "stumbling"? Simply put, what if being a "bad example" is not a bean in the bag? Land and Duke make clear the fact that people shouldn't think they are free to drink in their homes without consequence: "It is just nearly impossible to engage in this activity unobserved by someone." For them a Christian has no place in which he or she safely can drink alcohol without risking a negative result. In other words, the bean always is in the bag!

Regardless of insisting to the contrary, as many wisdom advocates do, conceiving circumstances so as not to offend a weaker brother by imbibing drink remains a possibility. The moderationists are right to point this out. The fact that the wisdom view may suffer inadequacy as a moral construct *standing alone* as it does becomes more evident. For the pond has been thoroughly drained all around as the wisdom view stands morally naked with nowhere to swim.

Unlike Land and Duke many wisdom advocates unfortunately make an even larger concession about the practice of Jesus. They concede Jesus *created* intoxicating wine, *consumed* intoxicating wine, and *commended* intoxicating wine. Some even go further and insist Jesus *commanded* intoxicating wine through the institution of the Lord's Supper.

From my viewpoint the effect of this concession cannot be overstated and stands as the Achilles' heel of those who hold this view. If those of us who desire to make a credible case for abstinence from intoxicating beverages must forfeit the example of our Lord Jesus, assuming He created as well as recreationally consumed the very substances from which we insist abstinence be observed, what possible moral ground do we have left? Do not the advocates for liberty in the responsible use of intoxicating beverages have a valid point? If we indict responsible drinking, we indict Jesus!

No biblical scholar to date has made this more clear than has 19th-century New Testament scholar Leon Field in his little book *Oinos: A Discussion of the Bible-Wine Question*: "The example of Christ must be regarded as determinative in this matter. If abstinence was his practice it is our duty. If moderation was his rule it may be our custom. To this extent we are in perfect accord with the [moderationists] just quoted. If their premises are correct their conclusion is inevitable. It is idle to deny this as many do" (Field, 1883).

In Part 3 much more will be said about our Lord and His view of wine. For now we'll content ourselves with simply asserting the absence of substantial reason—scriptural or otherwise—to accept as definitive the premise that Jesus created intoxicating wine or even consumed intoxicating wine for that matter.

In the end a better case for abstinence exists. It does not eliminate the wisdom view but embraces it, builds on it, and goes beyond it. We now grab our tools and begin to build.

Part 2

Chapter 9

"Drinking? No Way!"

We've arrived at a pivotal juncture in our quest for a broader, comprehensive moral construct for moderately consuming intoxicating substances strictly for pleasure. Obviously we've not seriously entertained the moral propriety of consuming intoxicants for medicinal purposes. Some seem to think embracing abstinence from intoxicating substances for the purposes of pleasure, if consistent, demands also the mistaken notion of abstinence from intoxicants altogether.

Medicinal purposes of alcohol irrelevant

For example many medicines contain alcohol; a fairly high percentage is found in some major brands of cough syrup. However, we've been careful to maintain when we are speaking of abstinence from intoxicants—including alcoholic beverages such as beer, wine, and whiskey—we're clearly referring to the hedonistic goal we call the *pleasurable consumption* of intoxicants. Common sense dictates a vast difference between guzzling beer with friends at the corner bar and swallowing two tablespoons of potent syrup to eliminate a hacking cough.

Therefore, we insist a clear distinction exists between *curing life*—which in many respects is enhanced with medicinal intoxicants—and *cultivating lifestyle,* which the pleasurable consumption of intoxicating substances enhances. The former undeniably concerns *health*; the latter unmistakably concerns *hedonism*. The hope of one *ends pain;* the hope of the other *enhances pleasure*. We might add, according to many interpreters, Scripture itself makes this fundamental distinction (1 Tim. 5:23). In the end, however, we entirely agree with Land and Duke in their observation about Southern Baptists: "As far as we know, no one in the Southern Baptist Convention would consider it sinful or inappropriate if someone drank these medications to help cope with the symptoms of a cold or flu." Thus, bringing up medicinal uses of intoxicants only muddies the water and avoids the real issue, which concerns the *recreational* use of intoxicants.

Introducing total abstinence

The stage is set for the final view—the view argued in the rest of the book—*total abstinence from intoxicating beverages for pleasurable purposes*. Of course this is no surprise, since in each chapter we've insisted on abstinence not only as a moral virtue but also as most consistent with Scripture, moral reasoning, historical context, and practical implementation.

We also note abstinence advocates and moderationists alike remain aware of the serious judgments many biblical passages make against drunkenness. Abstentionists are glad to agree. Even so, a systematic survey of the biblical texts relating to the subject reveals moderationists neglect to properly deal with the biblical texts that forbid not only the abuse of intoxicants leading to drunkenness but also, in some cases, forbid the use of wine altogether.

Also with those who embrace abstinence based on wisdom I am happy to unite. Even more I am glad to stand arm-in-arm against those who insist that drinking in moderation is perfectly acceptable and even a commendable moral practice in many respects. Nevertheless, we would neither be true to history, our understanding of Christian ethics, nor our conviction about biblical revelation if we stopped short of embracing principled abstinence derived from Scripture which *builds on*, but nonetheless, *goes beyond* the moral observation indicating abstinence to be a wise choice.

As I see it, to encourage our young generation to choose abstinence because abstinence is a wise choice has a morally hollow ring about it. Choosing college is a wise choice as well, but young collegians do not associate college as a wise choice with college as a moral choice. In my estimation the wisdom view standing alone hardly produces the moral torque required to hold the adventurous but fallen human spirit in check. Principled abstinence derived from Scripture offers greater thrust in constructing a moral standard for future generations of young people.

Abstinence is God's idea

The idea of abstinence is as old as the human race. God instituted abstinence apparently as the first injunction to the human pair He'd especially made in His own image. In her dialogue with the devil, who'd slithered in under the radar as a serpent, the mother of all living repeats verbatim God's vocal instruction: *But of the fruit of the tree which is in the midst of the garden, God hath said, Ye shall not eat of it, neither shall ye touch it, lest ye die* (Gen. 3:3). Clearly, the don't-eat-don't-touch structure of God's Word to Eve echoes for us the idea of abstinence. Abstinence, after all, is fundamentally a denial, a resistance, an inner vow one makes to one's self—and, in many cases, and more significantly to God—to avoid, to separate, in essence, to "not" whatever that "not" might be. For Eve it was "not eat" as well as "not touch." I suppose in one sense we could say abstinence is the principle of "not." And, when viewing "nots" in the case of morals, God Himself is the One who speaks them.

In addition these "nots" are interwoven throughout biblical revelation. As a matter of fact "nots" are codified in what both Jews and Christians reference as the Ten Commandments. Ever noted just how many "nots" are listed in the Ten Commandments? Here they are: not make, not bow, not take, not work, not kill, not adulterate, not steal, not lie, not covet

(Ex. 20:1-17). Each one of these "nots" requires practicing abstinence. On the one hand one abstains from making idols and abstains from worshiping them. On the other hand one abstains from both stealing things and coveting things. Thus, interwoven into the moral fabric of classic, Judeo-Christian ethics is the fiber we call *abstinence*.

This is not all. We find abstinence in the dietary laws of the Old Testament (Lev. 11:1-47). The formula found throughout this entire chapter is "eat" and "not eat." The former is clean food that may be eaten. The latter is unclean food from which they must abstain. Fish could be eaten, but the people must abstain from fowl. While we may wonder how or why God determines the distinction He makes between clean and unclean, the truth we seek does not depend on answers to those questions. Nor am I advocating the moral relevancy of dietary laws today (Mark 7:18-19). Rather the moral principle projected yet once again by the Almighty Himself is the principle of abstinence—abstaining from the unclean. Do we not see clearly that the larger, more fundamental moral grounding our Lord sought from His people when He instructed them in dietary restrictions concerned an inner principle—a vow to obey Him regardless of their physical preferences for food forbidden? He sought from them *abstinence*, did He not? He sought a human *yes* to abstain from the unclean. In this light abstinence becomes a pillar—a moral non-negotiable plank on which holiness to the Lord depends.

I might add that thus far no signs of moderation as a moral principle appear. God does not tell Adam and Eve to be moderate in their consumption of the fruit in question; God does not reveal through Moses for the people to worship Him exclusively but only moderately; God does not tell them to use moderation in their construction of idols; God does not reveal moderation as the key to truth-telling, stealing property, or coveting a neighbor's wife. Neither does God instruct His people to moderately distinguish between the clean and unclean

101

foods. Instead the moral principle we inevitably perceive—the yardstick by which moral behavior is always measured—appears to us in the absolute, not the relative; that is, in abstinence, not moderation, holiness not hedonism. The Almighty speaks. He speaks the only language sinful, rebellious humanity can understand. God speaks the language of abstention.

No less so do we find the abstinence principle within the confines of the New Testament. Beginning with the profound example the abstinence principle bears in John the Baptist we hear the angel declare: *For he shall be great in the sight of the Lord, and shall drink neither wine nor strong drink; and he shall be filled with the Holy Ghost, even from his mother's womb* (Luke 1:15). Even more our hearts melt when we connect both with the example and teaching our Lord Jesus gives us. That example and teaching bear the abstinence principle. Mark captures for us a glimpse into the Lord's practice of abstinence: *And immediately the spirit driveth him into the wilderness. And he was there in the wilderness forty days, tempted of Satan; and was with the wild beasts; and the angels ministered unto him* (Mark 1:12-13). Though Mark chooses not to fill in details about Jesus' dialogue with the devil—a dialogue possessing at least some strange similarity to the devil's long-ago conversation with Eve—we find from other Inspired sources one of the points of conversation: *And the devil said unto him, If thou be the Son of God, command this stone that it be made bread* (Luke 4:3). As with both Eve (Gen. 3:3) and Israel (Lev. 11:1-2) so similarly with our Lord, the occasion Satan first advances to challenge the Messiah tempts Him to deny abstinence and to indulge Himself. Such indulgence would relieve His vowed restraint from physical nourishment by breaching His inner abstinence but for spiritual nourishment. Yet unlike both Eve and Israel who abandon abstinence, selfishly indulging not only their outer cravings but their inner as well, the Word Who became flesh remains true to His higher need: *And Jesus answered him, saying, It is writ-*

ten, *That man shall not live by bread alone, but by every word of God* (Luke 4:4). During the entire 40-day period indulgence occurs, but it is indulgence in spiritual and not physical revelry. Our Lord focuses on hearing the Father, not heeding his senses; on fulfilling His eternal destiny, not fulfilling His temporary desire. For Christ, practicing abstinence remains a rule—a moral standard throughout His life.

The life Jesus lives, He lives hunkered down in holiness and is immovably attached to following His Father's will. *I have meat to eat ye know not of*, He tells His disciples on their insistence He eat. Looking at Him with no strangeness to spare they query whether any man has brought to Him bread. The Lord reveals to them both His abstinence and indulgence—*My meat is to do the will of him that sent me, and to finish his work* (John 4:32, 34). Indulging on one Manna meant abstaining from another.

Such is the way of Christ. His is the way of discipline—a life rooted deeply in a garden named *abstinence*. To say *yes* to Jesus is to say *no* to the world. Indulging in Him means abstaining from them. No person may re-create Him after his or her own hedonistic image—seeking pleasures below while abstaining from glory above. Indeed to suggest the philosophy of moderation—which inevitably focuses on amounts, not actions; on compromise, not commitment; on hedonistic lifestyle, not holy living—to suggest moderation connects neatly into our Lord's moral framework remains so absurd and so profoundly foreign to what the New Testament reveals about Him, one is tempted to conclude only hell itself is sophisticated enough to hatch such an interpretive hoax. In His life on earth Jesus practices the ethic of abstinence.

Abstinence is further evidenced in the teachings of Jesus. Far from the public displays of pious religion on which the Pharisees thrive, Jesus shocks His disciples with a distinctive didactic focus on secret prayer, which surely is a form of abstinence and definitive contrast to the hedonistic cravings the

Pharisees project as they seek gratification from others (Mt. 6:5-7). While Pharisees fill their outward cups and receive sinful but satisfying accolades, Jesus speaks of inward cups filled from the Father's fountain. But the inward cup is filled only in secret—alone and away from the crowds, impossible for pride-pursuing Pharisees whose hearts have never said *no* to the praise of men. The time finally arrives, however; Jesus calls His disciples down another avenue of prayer—an avenue of abstinence—the street called *No*. No praise from others means abstinence from others. Indulging in prayer means abstaining from people. The prayer-place to which our Lord bids us go is to abstinence—saying *No* to others, *No* to things, *No* to the world but *Yes* to Him.

Not only so, a more explicit expression of abstinence Jesus describes later on in His sermon: *Moreover when ye fast, be not, as the hypocrites, of a sad countenance: for they disfigure their faces, that they may appear unto men to fast. Verily I say unto you, They have their reward. But thou, when thou fastest, anoint thine head, and wash thy face; That thou appear not unto men to fast, but unto thy Father which is in secret: and thy Father, which seeth in secret, shall reward thee openly* (Mt. 6:16-18). Fasting's practice is but a snapshot—a moment in time reminding us our lives are built from the bottom up through abstinence. Through fasting we're painfully reminded the senses we deem, the tastes we develop, the satisfactions we deliver, the pleasures we desire, the preferences we decide are but passing, fading scenes as we slowly, steadily make our way up God's Mountain. Fasting stitches invisible threads to our inner souls, strengthens our resolve, and clinches us firmly to Christ's call, *Follow Me*. Is this so difficult to discern? Are our eyes hopelessly under this world's spell, as we are mesmerized by pleasure's well-proven potion? No one is beyond addiction to this world's magic. Even the strongest disciple denies three times. We, I assure, would deny four. And for what? A measly pauper's crumb of self-preservation, a cup of soup to satisfy our passing pride? *Why sleep ye?* says our Lord. Rise and pray! Rise? Pray? And even fast too? Is abstinence not what our Lord means? When our Lord says, *Moreover when ye fast . . .*, does He not mean "moreover when you abstain"?

And, concerning redemptive matters about which every person on the globe should possess interest, what does our Lord do but also, in a way only He can, pitch to us the principle of abstinence?

*And when he had called the people unto him with his disciples also, he said unto them, Whosoever will come after me, let him **deny** himself, and take up his cross, and follow me* (Mark 8:34 emphasis added here and below).

*Then said Jesus unto his disciples, If any man will come after me, let him **deny** himself, and take up his cross, and follow me* (Mt. 16:24).

*And he said to them all, If any man will come after me, let him **deny** himself, and take up his cross daily, and follow me* (Luke 9:23).

Can we possibly miss the meaning the Lord Jesus gives? Discipleship begins with denial; the act of denial captures the fundamental idea of abstinence. According to Jesus denying self is the bedrock spiritual demand to being His disciples. Indeed our discipleship to Jesus and His Lordship remains an inner faith-vow—a definitive abstinence from ourselves and our sinful, self-made lordship toward which we've so uncontrollably indulged our spiritual allegiance and left but a darkened, empty hull behind. Dietrich Bonhoeffer said, "When Christ calls a man, He bids him, 'Come and die'." The denying . . . the dying is nothing more or less than the principle of abstinence in its redemptive cloak. Discipleship begins with denial. Indeed in a real way discipleship is denial; discipleship is abstinence.

Make no mistake: the abstinence from self about which Jesus speaks remains fully absolute and is consistent with the abstinence principle we discover elsewhere in Scripture. Recall the warning Jesus offers to the one who lightly practices abstinence from self: *And Jesus said unto him, No man, having put his hand to the plough, and looking back, is fit for the kingdom of God* (Luke 9:62). Abstinence is the negative side of the moral hub situated in personal discipleship to Jesus, just as taking up one's assigned cross is the positive side of our discipleship to Jesus. Discipleship says *yes* to the demands of Jesus as Lord and *no* to the temptations of the world.

Discipleship, of course, begins with God's free grace in justification, as we place our faith in the atoning work of Christ's redemptive cross. Nevertheless, the grace of discipleship—*if it is truly God's grace and not some antinomian counterfeit*—necessarily proceeds from justification into sanctification and ultimately glorification. Biblical discipleship steers your life and connects your faith to live the life Christ offers—even Christ demands. It is a life of holiness—a faith fully realized, fully experienced. Our faith in the Lord Jesus seals us to the Father and secures us as living, breathing disciples of Jesus. As disciples—followers of Him—we flesh out biblical discipleship in holiness. As long as we're in the world, we're not to be of the world but victorious over the world. Abstinence remains crucial in doing so.

Conclusion

Were we of a mind to, we could continue to rewind and fast-forward back and forth from Old Testament to New Testament and choose from any number of moral concerns about which Scripture addresses and discover from the text the abstinence principle at the core. In other words abstinence appears to be the singular moral pattern when Scripture calls for moral practice and moral holiness. Consequently the pattern we discern makes the moral idea of moderation difficult to entertain. For us, accepting the consumption of addictive, demonstrably deadly intoxicants for the sheer purpose of social pleasure, so long as we don't overdo it, is morally absurd. In biblical categories a moral framework constructed on the rickety platform moderation offers remains destined to unconditionally collapse.

Therefore when we're speaking of consuming the various alcoholic products in today's market—a market whose self-perpetuating existence depends on keeping current customers and recruiting our sons and daughters as future drinkers—we insist moral reasoning, a decidedly Christian ethic, biblical wisdom, and, as we now shall see, a thoroughly biblical view of wine all point to one conclusion: *abstinence from intoxicating beverages for pleasurable purposes.*

Part 3

Chapter 10

What the Bible Says About Drink

We now begin an entirely new section that focuses specifically on what the Bible reveals about wine and wine products. Up until this point a conscious attempt has been made to gain a broader, deeper, and more comprehensive understanding of both abstinence as a moral construct—that is, an overarching absolute moral principle by which to live—and how applied abstinence affects the way one views the entire gamut of intoxicating substances available for consumption. The final section will limit itself to biblical revelation.

Let's be clear what our study is *not* about. Our study is not primarily focused on what the Bible says about drunkenness. Indeed no dispute exists so far as Christians are concerned about whether the Bible condemns drunkenness. The Bible does and does so indisputably. Drunkenness depends on our sinful flesh indicative of our own lives and not on our new life in Christ (Gal. 5:19, 21). Drunkenness is contrary to the Spirit and His leadership in our lives (Eph. 5:18). Finally, the Apostle Paul goes so far as to say the drunkard shall not inherit the Kingdom of God (1 Cor. 6:10).

Instead our study is much broader than centering on the effects of drinking. We're also concerned about what the Bible says about drink itself—that is, about the beverages and the fermented products of the grape that cause drunkenness. What the Bible says about fermented products in general will be key in developing a broad moral construct inclusive not only of alcoholic beverages on the market today but also of all intoxicating substances.

The haunting question for those who embrace abstinence
Most advocates who embrace moderate consumption of alcohol know the right question to pose to the unwary **abstentionist**: *"Just where does the Bible say 'thou shalt not consume alcohol'?"* Sometimes in a premature panic the shamed abstentionist slouches over and slowly slithers away defeated by the drinking apologist who's dead-sure the case for beverage alcohol has won the day. This scene sadly but repeatedly becomes the norm even in evangelical circles. What is one to think when the critic seems right? No Bible verse exists!

A more scholarly approach is offered by Adrian Jeffers, who writes in a much acclaimed essay by those who advocate consumption, " . . . Wine is good, it is a gift of God, if it is used in moderation . . . It is here, however, that this whole study comes to bear—what is the proper scriptural attitude toward a genuine believer who may drink an occasional glass of wine or bring home a 'six pack' . . .? Most of us would consign such (if it were in our power) to the lowest hell. But this would be contrary to the Bible, for no where does the Bible *command* total abstinence" (Jeffers, 1975).

More frustrating is the practice of some moderationists to admire the abstainer on one hand and ridicule him or her in the very next breath. One popular moderationist goes so far as to equate total abstinence from alcoholic beverages to doctrines inspired by the devil. He writes: "Those who desire to impose a law of total abstinence upon Christians are departing from the truth of God and following *the doctrine of demons . . ..* There is no greater need in the Church today than to reject this *doctrine of devils"* (Williamson, 1999). How his charge squares with the official stance of total abstinence from alcoholic beverages his denomination embraced a century ago I am unsure. The Presbyterian Church was broadly supportive of abstinence from recreational use of alcohol and even referred to liquor as the "devil's brew." Surely the Presbyterians never thought then that 100 years later one of their sons in the faith would accuse them of teaching "doctrines of devils" when teaching abstinence.

Wines then, wines today

Let's go back to the moderationist's question I mentioned above: *"Just where does the Bible say 'thou shalt not consume alcohol'?"* This question reveals more ignorance than confidence, I'm afraid. While few explicit injunctions against intoxicating substances such as alcohol in Scripture exist, the fact is, the Bible knows nothing of the modern alcoholic beverages produced today. Neither distillation nor pasteurization was known in biblical times. Distilled liquors weren't available until around the 15th century.

Furthermore, eminent French scientist Louis Pasteur didn't discover the scientific nature of fermentation until the 1860s (Bespaloff, 1988). Why would such be relevant? British theologian and pastor Peter Masters explains that in Bible times the highest achievable alcohol content of wines was around 14 percent. Yet "wine was not normally fermented anywhere near to that ceiling because of the unpleasant taste produced by extraneous bacteria which their technology could not eliminate." The result was sugar turned into vinegar; "while their strength is not known, the indications are that they were extremely weak" (Masters, 1992).

In other words neither distilled beers nor wines occurred to the authors when the biblical literature was written. For them wines primarily were for *food* and not *fun*. That is not to say wines were not prominently embedded in the culture then —both for celebration (weddings) and ceremony (worship). Like many other nations in the ancient era Israel remained a **viticulturally** driven nation. Grapes ruled! Just as the dollar drives our economic survival, so the grape and grape product drove their economic survival. This makes understanding the perpetual gratitude the ancient Hebrews expressed for the grape, the harvest, and the produce from the grape much easier. Psalm 104:14-15 says, *He causeth the grass to grow for the cattle, and herb for the service of man: that he may bring forth food out of the earth; And wine that maketh glad the heart of man, and oil to make his face to shine, and bread which strengtheneth man's heart.*

We'll look further on these verses later. The simple point to note now is, the prominence of the grape-driven economy cannot be overestimated as a backdrop in fully appreciating Israel's thanksgiving to God for the vineyard. Robert Teachout, in *The Use of Wine in the Old Testament*, his unpublished doctoral dissertation presented at Dallas Theological Seminary, explains about what he describes as the great cultural gap: "In modern American culture where . . . only a relatively few . . . raise the food supplies for the masses, it is difficult, if not impossible, for one to appreciate the joys of the less technological society whose life was so closely related to the soil" (Teachout, 1979). In other words the average family's personal experience today with harvest hardly extends beyond a visit to the produce section of the grocery store. By contrast Israel can be summarized by the phrase *each man under his own vine and fig tree* (1 Kings 4:25; Micah 4:4; Zech. 3:10). Consequently how easy but presumptuous for us, in reductionist fashion, to whittle down the ancient Hebrew's celebrative joy at harvest time for the abundant crop the Sovereign God graciously bestows on him, his family, and his people to a ridiculous giggly gratitude allegedly produced by a cup of fermented wine.

Was ancient Israel thankful for alcohol?

Unfortunately many moderationists claim that Israel offered its gratitude for precisely this "buzz" of alcohol.

Moderationists insist the actual stimulation on the human senses from the alcoholic substance itself is in view when wine *maketh glad* a person on consumption. Yet assuming that alcohol enhances joy—at least joy in any genuine biblical sense—is a mistake. In fact alcohol is a depressant; it dulls the senses and therefore diminishes what could be called a conscious enjoyment of the provision, despite any tipsy feeling to the contrary.

In an exchange he and I had over the verses above, one Southern Baptist pastor possessed no hesitation about stating precisely what he believed the Bible teaches us when it exhorts ancient Israel to gratitude for *wine that maketh glad the heart of man.* The pastor wrote, "*I do believe that alcohol was present here to gladden the heart of men. The wine had an effect on the person to gladden his heart and that was not seen as a bad thing in and of itself.*"

Kenneth Gentry, who may be the source most widely read by moderation advocates, seems to believe the exhilarating feeling from the alcohol entering the central nervous system is something for which to praise God. He writes: "A moderate gladdening of the heart was not forbidden, according to this and other scriptures" (Gentry, 2001). To suggest that an additive such as alcohol, consequent of the decay that takes place during fermentation and that is the responsible intoxicating agent, is primarily the object for which the Hebrew people offered thanksgiving cannot be seriously considered as either fitting the context of those verses or squaring with canons of common sense. Thanking God for intoxicating beverage is like thanking God for molded bread! This just doesn't add up.

Not only do we go against common sense to identify the primary object for which the Hebrew people offer gratitude to God for *wine that maketh glad the heart of man,* it also ignores the contextual setting within the psalm. Note again in verses 14-15 the several sources for which Israel is to be thankful. The people are to be grateful for the *grass* for the cattle and the *herb* for human service. The result is *food, wine, oil,* and *bread*. Apart from the wine, the other sources of happiness that are listed seem to possess a common thread–*naturally raw state*. And, even if one could argue that *food* and *bread* are not mentioned in their naturally raw states, neither should we assume that the psalmist is speaking of their *deteriorated* states either, which is precisely what fermented wine is—*deteriorated wine*.

What many fail to realize is that the natural fermentation of grapes does not lead to a drinkable beverage. Instead, uncontrolled it leads to a product unfit to consume. Natural fermentation is the second law of thermodynamics applicable to crushed grapes. Fermenting wine produces the horrid, foul odor of rot and decay—a particularly formidable challenge the ancients combatted. The fermentation process was carefully monitored and controlled, else the only product resulting would be soured vinegar impossible to drink and certainly nothing for which to *maketh glad the heart of man*.

So am I arguing that the Bible knows nothing of intoxication? No. Keep in mind the first mention of wine in the Bible is in conjunction with Noah's drunkenness (Gen. 9:20-25). The ancients knew very well the powers of fermented wine, though they neither knew what fermentation was (scientifically) or what the substance of alcohol was. In fact they had no word for *alcohol* in Hebrew or Greek. Consequently that's one reason the biblical authors, especially in the Old Testament, *describe* the effects of alcoholic wine rather than *define* alcoholic wine. Pertaining to another passage but just as applicable here, Old Testament scholar Stephen Reynolds writes, "Of course they knew of the intoxicating qualities of certain drinks, but this knowledge did not enter into their language in naming the beverages. It is for this reason that when God prohibited alcoholic drink in Proverbs 23:31-35, He had to describe its effects on the drinker, and, because He spoke to the people in the language they can understand, He could not prohibit alcohol in one word" (Reynolds, 2003).

Fermentation

So what is fermentation anyway? Fermentation is the process by which the sugar of the grape (obviously, in other fruits suitable for wine as well) is transformed into two substances: carbon-dioxide and ethanol; that is, alcohol (Bespaloff, 1988). The ratio is about dead-even: 50-percent carbon dioxide and 50-percent alcohol. Though obviously ancients knew about fermentation, they did not know what caused it and thought it was probably spontaneously generated. Thus in the ancient record the process of fermentation is not documented (Teachout, 1979).

Just how is the sugar transformed to carbon-dioxide and alcohol? Tiny single-cell microorganisms live on the grape skin. When the grape skin is pierced by any number of ways, the organisms get to the grape itself. The sugar supply is overrun by these outside invaders, whose sole purpose is to pillage the sugar. On contact the microorganisms—or if you prefer, *yeast cells*—release enzymes that in turn transform the sugar into gas and liquid alcohol—the stuff that makes you stagger! As for the gas think of Jesus' words about the bursting wineskins (cp. Mt. 9:17).

Again, even though the ancients knew nothing of why fermentation took place, they knew something of the process. Teachout explains the fermentation process beginning with filtering the wines. The filtering process included pouring the wine through linen cloths into containers. Afterward they poured the filtered wine into slender jars coated with resin. They sealed the jars with clay corks to hinder further fermentation and stored them in cool cellars. The entire process was elaborate, time-consuming, and had to be carefully maintained to keep the wine either fresh for immediate use or from turning to vinegar if the fermentation process got out of control.

The significance of words

Last fall my wife and I drove to the north Georgia

Mountains to attend an annual apple festival. I'm a sucker for fried apple pies (no sugar added) and fresh apple *cider*. I think I drank at least three servings of that stuff. Delicious! Now had I downed some ciders, I'd be down on my face and completely in a drunken stupor! Sometimes cider with such a quantum kick is qualified and dubbed *hard cider*. Nevertheless both beverages are well known and are routinely referred to simply as *cider*.

My experience above well illustrates in another way what Reynolds says above. The way most English Bibles translate the term *wine* is similar, if not identical, to the way we use *cider*. Varieties of wines are mentioned in the Old and New Testaments as Nehemiah makes clear when he mentions *all sorts of wine* (Neh. 5:18).

The term *wine* in the English Bible represents a virtual baker's dozen of both Hebrew and Greek words with meanings ranging from the vineyard itself (Judg. 9:13; Ps. 4:7) to freshly-squeezed grape juice in the cup to be consumed immediately (Deut. 32:14). *Wine* is the product squeezed into the vat as men crush the grapes (Joel 2:24; Prov. 3:10). Scripture speaks of wine products most probably stored in such a way to hinder as much as possible any fermenting. Of course the Bible makes abundantly clear that wine products are intoxicating products.

The term *wine*, therefore, as used in our English Bible, is to be regarded as a generic term comprehending different kinds of beverage and of different qualities, some of which kinds were good, some bad; some to be used frequently and freely, some seldom and sparingly; and some to be utterly and at all times avoided (Nott, 1857). Nevertheless, the English word translated for each of these meanings normally and overwhelmingly is the word *wine*. Should we be surprised we're many times confused about what the Bible teaches about wine?

Lees and Burns translate Nehemiah's *all sorts of wines* literally as "with every (sort of) wine abundantly," "a copious supply of all kinds of wine" (Lees, Burns, & Lewis, 1870). They further remark, "No fact is better established in regard to ancient times than the great diversity of their vinous preparations, a diversity extending not only to the modes of their manufacture, but to their qualities and effects . . . Some might be new, some old; some pure, some mixed; some fresh from the vat, some boiled; some watery, some thick; some sweet as honey, others thin and tart."

The masterful exegete and scholar Adam Clarke notes: "The Hebrew, Greek, and Latin words which are rendered 'wine,' mean simply the expressed juice of the grape." Hence, we find that different words in the Bible are translated *wine*, which once again proves that *wine* is a generic term and covers the stages of all sorts of wine spoken of in Nehemiah. John Ellis, writing in the late 19th century, said, "At the present day, also, the term [wine] is used in precisely this [generic] manner. It may mean grape, currant, raspberry, whortleberry, elderberry, madeira, port, cherry, and a hundred other wines. It may refer to new, old, sweet, sour, weak, or strong wines. It may refer to enforced or unenforced, fermented or unfermented wine" (Ellis, 1882).

At first the Old Testament's reservoir of words (nine in all), all of which inevitably end up being translated *wine,* may not seem as though it is a big deal. This wouldn't be nearly as significant if the English term *wine* itself had not changed. The fact remains: the overwhelming majority of people today assume *wine* categorically refers to an alcoholic beverage. Indeed most insist *wine* can refer only to fermented, intoxicating beverages. But as Robert Teachout explains, people have taken the *usual* definition of the word *wine,* which surely refers to fermented, intoxicating grape juice and taken that definition as the *only definition* of the word.

The 1828 Webster's Dictionary defines the term *must* as wine pressed from the grape but not *fermented.* Thus, here's one 19th-century linguistic source that explicitly speaks of *unfermented wine.* The 1759 New Universal English Dictionary of Words and of Arts and Sciences defines *wine* as follows: "Natural wine is such as it comes from the grape, without any mixture or sophistication. Adulterated wine is that wherein some drug is added to give it strength, fineness, flavor, briskness, or some of the qualification" (Bacchiocchi, 2004). Note the distinction in the definition between the *natural wine,* where no hint of fermentation exists, and the *adulterated wine,* which obviously includes intoxication.

Benjamin Marin's *Lingua Britannica Reformata or a New English Dictionary* (1748) defines the primary meaning of *wine* as "the juice of the grape." Again, no mention of fermentation appears. However, of interest in this particular dictionary is the secondary meaning: "the vapours of wine, as wine disturbs his reason", a clear reference to intoxicating qualities but used only in the secondary sense. At least as far as this reference goes, *wine* in the unfermented, non-intoxicating variety of pure grape juice seems to have possessed at least an equal and perhaps even a superior usage in the English language.

One wine or two?

This brief survey of both biblical and English words that communicate to us through the term *wine* is of course not meant as an exhaustive study. Instead it stands as a necessary background for the reader to grasp the richness and in many ways the complexity of the study of *wine* in Scripture. Furthermore this leads us to a major question about our understanding of intoxicating drink. The truth be told, the majority of Christians assume when the Bible speaks of *wine,* no matter the passage in which the term is found, the inevitable assumption brought to the text and the inevitable conclusion taken away from the text is that the *wine* mentioned is an intoxicating, alcoholic substance. Indeed this assumption may be the key to filtering out some of the confusion about the biblical understanding of wine.

Does the Bible reveal only one type of wine? Or does a variety of wines within the context of Scripture exist? From the evidence we presented above, the answer to the first question seems to be an emphatic *No*, while the answer to the second question is an obvious *Yes*. In Scripture what we have is a variety of wines, from freshly-squeezed grape juice to be immediately consumed and enjoyed to wines that are mixed and that contain additives that may even accelerate the intoxicating effect. Once again Robert Teachout in his exhaustive study of wine in the Old Testament suggests that of the hundreds of references in the Old Testament just more than half refer to unfermented, non-intoxicating wine products.

Admittedly this idea appears foreign to many. Indeed even many studied men and women immediately will question this assertion. Of course, in itself that should be a good thing. This particular area of scholarship has been dormant far too long.

Interestingly the biblical scholars about whom we spoke leading up to Prohibition were virtually united in their interpretation of the biblical record, which they interpreted to reveal two kinds of wine—freshly-squeezed, unfermented grape juice known as *wine* and also fermented, intoxicating wine. Mention today that the Bible reveals two broad categories of wine; one may expect either ridicule or a blank stare to follow. Nonetheless some of the most renown exegetes interpreted Scripture as revealing varied wines.

John J. Owen's prolific writings in theology and biblical exposition were mainstays for pastor and scholar alike all across the globe in the 19th century. Indeed today he still remains valuable in many ways. In his commentary on Jesus' first miracle in John's gospel Owen writes that the wine was the "pure juice of the grape" that was "wholly free from the alcoholic stimulant". He concludes, "No plea whatever can be justly drawn from it, for the use of such adulterated and poisons [sic] wines, as are generally imported and vended in this country" (Owen J.J., 1860). Owen further said about the drinking practices of Jesus: "As wine was a common beverage in that land of vineyards, in its unfermented state, our Lord most likely drank it. But that he did so in its intoxicating forms, or that he indulged to excess in its use in any form, was a false and malicious libel upon his character" (Owen J., 1870).

Anglican theologian and biblical expositor Robert Maguire wrote of the difference between the wines of the Bible and wines since: "wine of the present day . . . cannot even rank among the ordinary wines of Scripture; and it is only in *name*, but certainly not in *nature*." Arguing his case on the basis of the different kinds of wine clearly embedded in Hebrew and Greek languages, Maguire further noted that the modern drinks in his day were, in their fiery, intoxicating, alcoholic nature, "so entirely differ from anything known or drank as a stimulant in the days of Scripture, that any passages of the sacred volume which appear to favor the use of the latter can be no honest interpretation be applied to the former. The drinks sanctioned in Scripture have now positively no existence among us" (Maguire, 1863).

The list seems endless—Adam Clarke, Albert Barnes, Thomas Scott, Ralph Wardlaw, F. R. Lees, James Smith, George Duffield, Dawson Burns, Tayler Lewis, William Patton, G. W. Samson, Moses Stuart, Canon F.W. Farrar, Alonzo Potter, G. Bush, and Norman Kerr—all of whom were eminent scholars of the 19th century. All these, along with the expositors already mentioned, understood Scripture to explicitly reveal both fermented and unfermented wines. Thus, when abstentionists suggest wine's dual nature being both freshly-squeezed grape juice as well as strong intoxicating beverage, know we're not pulling a hermeneutical rabbit out of the hat. A long, rich, and varied heritage is easily documented in church history.

Historical references outside the Bible

While our focus in this section primarily concerns wine in the Bible, one would be surprised, to say the least, if the understanding of wine and its products found in cultures parallel to those we find in Scripture is not similar to and arguably identical with Scripture itself. In short, if we find both kinds of wine in Scripture — that is, intoxicating and non-intoxicating varieties — the fact that we also find both kinds of wine outside the Bible only makes sense. After all wine and the wine product are natural resources indigenous to that part of the world. Consequently the measures and means by which the Hebrew people harvested their crops would overlap considerably with other cultures.

In addition not only would the very same products from the grape be available to all, but also the harvesting methods, processing, and preserving procedures of the grape and grape product would extend along the same lines. Such is precisely what we find when we scour the historical record. For example the Greek philosopher, Aristotle, in speaking of sweet wine, writes "that sweet wine [*oinos*, the Greek term used throughout the New Testament for wine] would not intoxicate."

Again, note Nicander, the Greek poet and physician of the second century B.C.: "And Cenus having squeezed the juice of the grapes, into hollow cups, called it wine (*oinos*)" (Nott, 1857). Thus, from both Aristotle and Nicander as sources, one is hardly justified in tacitly assuming *wine* always means intoxicating beverage. Juice squeezed into the cup for immediate consumption is termed *oinos* [*wine*] (see Appendices for more historical evidence).

Conclusion

Given the impressive evidence to the contrary, how we manage to possibly assume *wine* in Scripture necessarily and always refers to intoxicating beverages remains inexplicable. Indeed this may be the grandest hermeneutical hoax of the ages. We believe the simple observation that when the Bible speaks of *wine*, the fact that this does not necessarily refer to intoxicating wine fundamentally corrects the bias almost universally imbedded in the evangelical world. As the evidence demonstrates, the ancients employed painful, meticulous means to keep some wines from fermenting to the point of being toxic. *They desired pure, unfermented grape juice.* The evidence seems overwhelming. From my view, to deny it and argue to the contrary the premise that whenever the Bible speaks of *wine,* it always refers to intoxicating wine makes no reasonable sense and smacks of self-satisfied incoherence.

Essentially, while God gave wine for the enjoyment of people—to make them happy, to give them life (Ps. 104:14-15), not one shred of evidence compels us to believe the Bible is undeniably speaking of intoxicating drink. The ethyl alcohol in wine produced from the natural fermentation of the harvested grape is a form of *deterioration*—decay, if you will—in the very same sense that mold on bread is produced from the natural fermentation of the grain. *To be thankful for alcoholic wine is the exact equivalent of being thankful for molded bread!*

When God exhorts thanksgiving for wine, the people are not to be thankful about the beverage *per se;* most certainly it is not for the *decayed* beverage. Rather the admonition is given to a people who rely, for their survival, on the grape harvest. That is, *ancient Israel was particularly a society driven by viticulture*—something we cannot overlook when we study the biblical view of drink.

On the other hand when the Bible says, *Wine is a mocker, strong drink is raging: and whosoever is deceived thereby is not wise* (Prov. 20:1), what is to be our response? When Scripture says pointedly, *Look not thou upon the wine when it is red, when it giveth his colour in the cup, when it moveth itself aright* (Prov. 23:31), should we believe that this wine that mocks, rages, and deceives—the wine we're commanded not only not to drink but not even touch or look on—is the same wine for which the worshiper is to offer thanksgiving to God? (Ps. 104:14-15). The wine God condemns and warns against as a serpent that bites and injects its deadly poison into one's body (Prov. 23:32-33) is a wine we're convinced God does not approve. We think moderationists embrace a blatant contradiction and attempt to solve the dilemma by reading "moderate consumption" into the texts.

The wine for which, in the Scripture, Israel is to be thankful is the wine God commends for the people's sustenance, their survival, and their joy, and indicates His abundant blessing. Gratitude for this wine has absolutely nothing to do with its intoxicating effects. To the contrary the vineyard, the harvest, the cluster of grapes, the sweet fruit, and the fresh juice is what is to be celebrated as God's continued provision for His people. As Robert Maguire puts it, such "would seem to account for the diverse testimony of Scripture regarding wines; and that when the Bible commends the drinking of wine, as *making glad the heart of man* and otherwise contributing to his strength and vigor, it speaks of the native fruit of the vine pressed into the wine-cup; and, when it speaks in terms of admonition in warning and calls wine a 'mocker' and makes it the chosen symbol of the wrath of God and the pouring out a Divine vengeance, it indicates the harmful wine, fermented and adulterated."

Thus the distinction between intoxicating wine and non-intoxicating wine remains both valid and necessary to fully understand what the Bible says to us today about intoxicating beverages. Also, making this distinction assists in deflating and therefore minimizing any particular bias that is brought to the text of Scripture. How so? Because not only does it assist the interpreter when he or she reads the term *wine* to not assume the product is intoxicating or non-intoxicating, it forces the interpreter to examine the passage carefully and discover from the context itself whether the author means the grape product is intoxicating.

Many passages will be easy to ascertain the toxic nature of wine (Gen. 9:21). Others will be easy to see the innocence of wine (Ps. 104:14-15). As in every subject within the scope of

Scripture itself, passages exist that will be difficult to discern. Whether the wine to which the passage refers is intoxicating or not may not be perfectly clear. Our hope is as we interpret the Word of God, we will be faithful to the text the Holy Spirit inspired.

Finally we note our unwavering commitment to biblical inerrancy as the fundamental backdrop to biblical hermeneutics. Given our view of the God-breathed text of Scripture, we employ the *principle of interpretative harmonization*—that is, we do not believe Scripture contradicts Scripture. For example if Scripture in one place teaches that God is Spirit but in other places speaks of God's hands, God's eyes, God's fingers, etc., we do not believe the biblical text fundamentally contradicts itself. Instead reasonable answers more faithful to biblical revelation are easily discernable. Or if one gospel writer records one angel at Jesus' tomb and another gospel writer records two angels, we do not believe the difference equals contradiction (if two angels were there, logic demands that one was!). Rather the principle of harmony—with inerrancy as the backdrop—seeks an answer consistent with the God-breathed nature of the Bible.

Similarly what we find in Scripture is two apparent contradictory views of wine. On the one hand we see wine [*yayin*] being both praised and commended (Ps. 104:14-15). On the other we observe wine [*yayin*] being both treacherous and condemned. (Prov. 20:1). In fact some wine [*yayin*] is so lethal, God says to *look not upon it* (Prov. 23:31). We're convinced that to overlook this explicit tension is a mistake. We further believe to overlay an interpretative film onto these texts that reads "moderate consumption" into them not only does not lessen the tension; it offers false comfort for those who desire to imbibe alcoholic products.

Therefore, we insist that the consistency of God's Word is at stake in how we answer this question. No one said this more clearly than did Moses Stuart: "My final conclusion is this;

viz, that wherever the scriptures speak of wine as a comfort, a blessing, or libation to God, and rank it with such articles as corn and oil, they mean—they can mean—*only such wine as contained no alcohol that could have a mischievous tendency;* that wherever they denounce it, prohibit it, and connect it with drunkenness and revelling, they can mean only *alcoholic or intoxicating wine* . . . I cannot refuse to take this position without virtually impeaching the Scriptures of contradiction or inconsistency. I cannot admit, that God has given liberty to persons in health to drink alcoholic wine, without admitting that his word and his works are at variance" (Stuart, 1848).

Part 3

Chapter 11

The Old Testament and Drink

One of the difficulties in dealing with *wine* in the Bible is the astounding number of passages that mention the vineyard, the grape, the harvest, the processing, and end product of the fruit of the vine. Nevertheless, if we can gain a solid grasp on a few substantial passages, such an interpretive foundation will pay us untold dividends as we look at the larger scope of biblical revelation. With that in mind we're going to begin in Proverbs. Indeed no better place exists than the Book of Proverbs for us to gain the attitude of God Almighty toward wine. Why? Two reasons.

First, in Proverbs we find the perfect illustration of two entirely different kinds of wines biblically considered. Understanding that when the Bible speaks of *wine,* the fact that the term is used in a generic sense remains vital to grasping the full biblical scope of what the Bible teaches about wine. The famed Baptist scholar G. W. Samson wrote, "the Hebrew word *yayin* [translated *wine*] is without question generic, rather than special, including many species of wines that have more or less of the intoxicating quality" (Samson, 1880).

In perfect harmony with Samson was the eminent Andover scholar and theologian Moses Stuart, who wrote one of the most influential documents of the 19th century on this very question. In a letter to Eliphalet Nott he writes without vagary:

"there are, in the Scriptures, two generic words to designate such drinks as may be of an intoxicating nature when fermented, and which are not so before fermentation. In the Hebrew Scriptures, the word *yayin* in its broadest meaning designates grape-juice or the liquid which the fruit of the vine yields. This may be new or old, sweet or sour, fermented or unfermented, intoxicating or unintoxicating . . . It follows now, without any reasonable question, if the *yayin* be generic . . . It may designate any particular kind of wine . . . " (Stuart, 1848).

We need to point out that when we assert the generic use of *wine* in Scripture, we're not exercising a special rule of interpretation for the term *wine*. As a matter of fact many words in Scripture are generic in nature. For example in Genesis 1:1 the Hebrew term *elohim* refers to the one true and living God, while in Exodus 12:12 the same term *elohim* refers to the polytheistic gods of Egypt. Furthermore the same term, *elohim*, refers to angels! (Ps. 8:5; cp. Heb. 2:7) (Reynolds, 2003).

Nineteenth-century scholar William Ritchie incisively asks, "If we want to know whether water spoken of is salt water or fresh, rain-water or spring-water, it is of no purpose to be told that it is *water*. In this case, we should look with a good deal of astonishment at a person who might assure us there can be no doubt it is *salt* water, for is it not declared to be *water*?" (Ritchie, 1866). The same is true when we look at wine in the Bible. It is not enough to be told "it's wine, that's all." Yes, but what *kind* of wine?

Second, as the central book within the canonical writings we know as "Wisdom Literature", Proverbs offers us precisely what God considers righteous living. As we shall see, wisdom in Proverbs is not about wise choices. Surely this sounds confusing for us today, as often as we tell our children to "make wise choices." Or, we characterize the trouble a teen-ager experienced by suggesting he or she is reaping the results of "an unwise choice."

One thing to realize as we study Proverbs is the fact that wisdom is not mere knowledge; instead, wisdom in Proverbs is about pursuing life—*skill in practicing holiness* before the Lord (Teachout, 1979). Wisdom applies the knowledge of God and His standards to one's lifestyle. It connects such to the moral construct God demands from us. Consequently, since Wisdom is a primary attribute of God personified (Prov. 8:22-31), God's *righteous* acts are considered *holy* acts—*wise* acts. In other words *wisdom*, so to speak, is God's *skill in practicing His holiness*. In essence *wisdom* is living life after God.

In light of this, Proverbs may receive a long-overdue face-lift for some. It offers fresh moral exhortation to pursuing the wisdom life, which is nothing less, in the end, than pursuing a holy life. From God's standpoint His wisdom is His holiness!

Understandably this poses an immediate dilemma for those who've simplistically drained the moral authority bone-dry from God's wisdom sayings and left little behind but the dust of a conveniently wise nonetheless perfectly optional choice. For if we consider wisdom as God considers wisdom, Solomon's most famous proclamation that wine is *mocker,* that *strong drink* rages away, and that the one deceived *is not wise* rapidly accelerates to its full moral thrust—that the one deceived *sins against God.*

Illustrating the issue: two kinds of wine in Proverbs

In the Old Testament are nine Hebrew words that in the English Bible usually are translated *wine.* Sometimes God praises wine and gives it to His people in abundance and in a variety of ways. This creates joy in their lives as His people (Ps. 104:14-15). In addition a few times *wine* appears as the personified enemy of God's people (Prov. 20:1).

So far as *wine* in Proverbs goes, no less than 11 times is the term translated *wine* employed. And, behind the English term *wine,* two Hebrew words are used. The first word translated wine—*tirosh*—is used in only one proverb: *So shall thy barns be filled with plenty, and thy presses shall burst out with new wine [tirosh]* (Prov. 3:10). Let's make a few notes here.

First, the promise God offers supposes that the worshiper honors the Lord from the choicest pickings of the personal harvest (Prov. 3:9). This is when God gives the promise to abundantly bless. Their storage barns will burst with an over-abundance of grain that easily would last until next harvest. Also, their *yeqeb* will be filled with new wine. The word *yeqeb*, translated *presses* or *vats*, could be used as part of the wine press itself or of special storage containers for the freshly harvested grape produce. Since *barns* are for storing fresh grain (Prov. 3:10), consistency pushes us to see *vats* for storing fresh *tirosh* [wine].

Secondly, the *tirosh* translated *new wine* is definitively a freshly harvested produce that is stored in its naturally raw condition in the same way as was the grain. That does not mean no measures are taken to protect the fruit of the harvest from spoiling. Indeed we must presume Israel, like her surrounding neighbors, employed similar means to ensure the longevity of both grain and grape.

Incidentally, some make the naïve assumption the ancients knew absolutely nothing about how to preserve the raw grape and the grape's juice. In other words the fermentation process naturally led to fermented wine. All one had to do was wait. Abracadabra—they would have wonderfully smooth, delicious, and refreshing beverage. Of course it was alcoholic, but at least it was natural and it was good. Nonetheless, because of its naturally developed state of fermentation, they had to practice moderation in drinking it.

The fact is, however, fermented wine, apart from sophisticated measures to control the process, would not be vintage brew. Rather wine naturally fermented apart from human intervention would be vinegar—an undrinkable, spoiled liquid only good for one thing: pitch it out and consider that part of the harvest lost.

Ancient writers such as Cato, Columella, and Pliny speak of various ways that fermented, alcoholic wines were preserved from going bad (see Appendices). Sometimes they added sea water, resin, salt, or marble dust. Sometimes they would have to boil the fermented wine down to an almost clay-like substance to salvage any use at all. If they did not keep tight restrictions on the fermented wine, it would become infected with mold. Consequently it would become so acidic it would be unfit for human consumption.

Not to mention the fermented wine that became "foul" reeked with the smell of rotting corpses—a dead giveaway to prospective buyers that the merchants possessed a bad brew they were attempting to pawn off. *How amazing that moderationists continue to insist that God gives this fermented wine as a gift to His people to enjoy.* Hardly. God gives *tirosh—the harvest, the produce, the fruit of the grape—*to His people for which they are ever to offer thanksgiving to Him as Lord of the harvest. And He promises to fill their vats to overflow if they honor Him with their harvest's first fruits (Prov. 3:10).

The second word in Proverbs translated in English Bibles as *wine* is *yayin*. *Yayin* stands without controversy as the most well-worn word for *wine* in the entire Old Testament. It was employed no less than a staggering 141 times and translated *wine*. The word *yayin* stands central as we attempt to understand "wine" in the Old Testament. Primarily two reasons exist (Teachout, 1979). First is the frequency of *yayin* occurring in Scripture—fully 141 times. Such frequency itself makes it of special interest.

Also, we note the dual way in which the word is used. Robert Teachout writes, "Sometimes [*yayin*] receives the approbation of God and other times it bears only His wrath." Furthermore Teachout goes on to remind us that *yayin* permeates the entire Old Testament revelation. It appears thoroughly in each type of literature, in each chronological period, and in all but seven canonical books (Ruth, 1 and 2 Kings, Obadiah,

Jonah, Nahum and Malachi).

We also point out that almost all agree *yayin* [wine] receives God's approval in Scripture. Some assume those advocating abstinence do not appreciate the myriad passages in which *wine* [*yayin*] is viewed as positive (cp. Ps. 104:14-15). As we've shown above, this assumption is thoroughly mistaken. What abstentionists insist on, however, is taking just as seriously those passages in which *wine* [*yayin*] is condemned.

Furthermore, many who advocate the moderate consumption of alcohol not only outright dismiss passages denouncing consumption of intoxicants but subtly overlay onto the text of Scripture a film through which they view the text. For them, whenever wine [*yayin*] is mentioned in the Old Testament—indeed in all of God's Word, including *oinos* [wine] in the New Testament—only one kind of wine exists: *intoxicating wine*. We recognize the repetitive practice of mentioning this so often; however, in my view, the significance of this cannot be overestimated.

Precisely here is where the moderationist and those who hold to total abstinence part ways. For while abstentionists can wholeheartedly agree with moderationists that God gave wine for us to enjoy, moderationists cannot at all concede what Teachout mentioned above: "Sometimes [*yayin*] . . . bears only His wrath." In fact moderationists deny God's disapproval of wine period. Rather they focus on partaking of intoxicating beverages in controlled doses so as to avoid drunkenness, a moral principle we saw in **Part 1** more at home in Greek philosophy than biblical faith.

Nor has any moderationist we know explained precisely where Scripture explains how one knows when one is practicing moderation. What is the degree of intoxication to which one looks as a yardstick to measure when crossing from moderate drink to non-moderate drink? John L. Dagg (1794–1884), the first writing Southern Baptist theologian, was only 14-

years old when he left home and entered the work force. At his parting he records the warning his father gave him. His father urged him to be guarded against the temptation of imbibing ardent spirits. Later in his life when he was young in the ministry, he further records the first controversy he experienced with other Baptists. The controversy was over imbibing alcohol. On one occasion he asked, "At what point between total abstinence from ardent spirits, and intoxication by them, does the use of them become sinful?" The question received a stone-cold silence (Dagg, 1857). Dagg's question remains unanswered.

The moderation solution, I might add, is an easy solution but a dangerous one. It is dangerous because of the underestimation of the powerful addictive qualities of the drug alcohol; dangerous because moderation is not a universal solution for everyone—children, persons with addictive-oriented personalities, former drug addicts—and thus a moral ethic practicable for only certain people; dangerous because of no authoritative, biblical guidance establishing exactly what moderation is, leaving one to one's self in establishing an arbitrary guideline; and most of all, dangerous because moderation is neither necessary nor adequate in explaining those passages of Scripture that clearly state, "Sometimes [*yayin*] . . . bears only His wrath."

In summary *tirosh* refers primarily to the natural produce given as a blessing from God. *Yayin* refers to the actual consumable beverage. It is what is "in the grape", that which is squeezed out "in the press", that which is squeezed out "in the cup", the liquid that is stored "in the vat" and all this regardless of whether freshly produced or aged and fermented. Out of the 141 times *yayin* is used in the Old Testament, the usage is virtually split down the middle between *yayin* that is intoxicating and *yayin* that is fresh grape juice. Interestingly a slight edge is given to fresh grape juice (Teachout, 1979).

Proverbs 23:29-35: accepting the absolute prohibition

Perhaps the most familiar text about wine in the Old Testament, a least in the Wisdom literature, is Proverbs 23:29-35. Following is the entire passage:

29Who hath woe? who hath sorrow? who hath contentions? who hath babbling? who hath wounds without cause? who hath redness of eyes? 30They that tarry long at the wine; they that go to seek mixed wine. 31Look not thou upon the wine when it is red, when it giveth his colour in the cup, when it moveth itself aright. 32At the last it biteth like a serpent, and stingeth like an adder. 33Thine eyes shall behold strange women, and thine heart shall utter perverse things. 34Yea, thou shalt be as he that lieth down in the midst of the sea, or as he that lieth upon the top of a mast. 35They have stricken me, shalt thou say, and I was not sick; they have beaten me, and I felt it not: when shall I awake? I will seek it yet again.

First, observe the description of the *internal* effects of drinking habits. This is especially notable in the series of rhetorical questions that possesses an expected answer: *Who hath woe? who hath sorrow? who hath contentions? who hath babbling? who hath wounds without cause? who hath redness of eyes?* (v. 29). Who is the one who experiences sorrow, possesses troubles, and is ever caught a contentious spirit? And who might that be, Solomon inquires? Who is this person who chronically complains, feels wounds but cannot recall the cause, whose eyes reflect what his heart desires? Solomon is not shy in speaking this poor soul's name. He is the one who lingers or tarries *long* at the *yayin*. Lees translates this literally as those "tarrying (staying behind) at the wine" (Lees, Burns, & Lewis, 1870). The idea is one who enjoys wine's company—who cannot seem to leave wine's presence. Thus he stays behind to be alone with his friend, his friend whose name is *yayin*.

Note, the idea is absent that this lover's problem is that he is immoderate. To the contrary he is only in love. This is the description of a soap opera—a flirting with the one he loves. The problem is, the *yayin* for which his romance is stayed cannot satisfy his thirst. He neither lays in a drunken stupor nor wastes away in a pitiful mindset. Rather he rises and seeks out another lover—a lover whose promise offers him more than he ever dreams. He, then, goes on a journey, a quest for mixed wine— *they that go to seek mixed wine* [*mimsak*].

This term translated *mixed wine* is used only twice in the Old Testament (cp. Isa. 65:11-12). Sometimes "mixed wines" are not necessarily intoxicating in nature (Prov. 9:1-6). However, no mistaking the quest this wine-lover is pursuing. The Hebrew literally reads *to those going to search out mixture.* The thing that is sought is not stated. Presumably drugs are what makes *yayin* even more potent than it already has become. Thus we are introduced by Solomon to the internal struggles of one who is in love with *yayin* and the external, visible signs of his affair.

Solomon is not finished with the picture he wishes to draw for the unwary victim—the *external* effects he now must describe. Fast forwarding to verse 33, we find the man after he's found that for which he searches and the love for which he longs—*mimsak*—*yayin* mixed with other potencies. The result at last—*Thine eyes shall behold strange women, and thine heart shall utter perverse things.* Deception awaits. Direction is lost. Morals are depleted. One thing he has on his mind. It is not God. It is not hope. It is not purpose. It only is another drink.

Sandwiched between the internal and external signs of a man in love with *yayin* and the consequence of that love is Solomon's description of the deceiver, which he elsewhere terms a *mocker* and *brawler*—that which the very wisdom of God says do not partake (20:1). *Yayin* is what is forbidden to Kings, lest their sense of judgment vanishes (31:4-5); *yayin* that, in stark irony, is offered only to those whose lives mean nothing, whose hope is gone (31:6-7); *yayin* in the poison of snakes; *yayin* in the stings of adders (v. 32).

Without the least hesitation . . . without doubt . . .without embarrassment whatsoever Solomon says this *yayin* is the substance whose presence only the fool would offer a glance toward. He plainly offers this bit of Inspired Wisdom, a divine call to holiness—*Look not thou upon the wine [yayin]. Look not* is neither difficult to understand nor does it require special knowledge to grasp the meaning—*Do not look on the yayin.*

Once again noticeably absent is the mention of moderately looking at the wine. Nor is the mention here of drinking but not being drunk. No limitation to a single glass of wine is instructed. No mention of quantity, measure, or amount. Yet some see the solution to be in the *abuse* of *yayin* and not the *use* of *yayin*. Does Solomon mention abusing the wine? Using the wine? Does he not clearly demand that people not even look on the *yayin*? In the end one must ask whether *abuse* of *yayin* was Solomon's solution or a solution imposed on Solomon?

What does God instruct Lot? *Look not behind thee . . .* the Angel warns (Gen. 19:17). Do we suppose he means look a little? Can the Lord of hosts have meant, "You can use your eyes but not abuse your eyes"? Is looking a good thing just as long as you don't look too much? Perhaps Lot's wife thinks such is precisely what God means when He says *look not*. And, what may we ask, does Lot's wife do? Moses writes: *But his wife looked back from behind him, and she became a pillar of salt* (Gen. 19:26). In this context we don't think we're asking too much to recall the words of the Lord Jesus, *Remember Lot's wife* (Luke 17:32).

Surely some mystery remains about this wine on which we are not to look. *When it is red* is taken by some scholars to mean its deep color because of its age. *When it sparkles in the cup* means literally "when it gives in the vessel its eye." This very well could refer to its fizz as fermentation peaks or the bubble when the carbonic acid is produced.

When it moveth itself aright or goes down smoothly is troublesome but may best be seen as the ripples in the glass, again indicative of heightened fermentation. Whatever these particulars are, we are certain of one thing: The *yayin* about which Solomon warns is potent, dangerous, deadly, and ends in destruction—that is, *the bite of a cobra.* From my understanding of this passage little hope exists apart from denying its reality that Solomon means to portray that drinking this wine he describes in small portions is acceptable. To do so will be irresponsibly playing with a cobra whose one single bite is the bite of death.

Proverbs 9:1-6

As noted earlier Proverbs offers definitive examples that show the generic use of *yayin* [*wine*] in Scripture. As we shall see below, *yayin* [*wine*] can be viewed as a beverage to enjoy not in moderation but rather to full indulgence, expecting it to give life, satisfaction, and wisdom. Such is in direct contrast to the very same drink [*yayin, wine*] as a mocker, a drink of rage and deception, and a serpent with a deadly bite to be shunned at all costs we've seen above (20:1; 23:31-32).

Wisdom hath builded her house, she hath hewn out her seven pillars: She hath killed her beasts; she hath mingled her wine; she hath also furnished her table. She hath sent forth her maidens: she crieth upon the highest places of the city, Whoso is simple, let him turn in hither: as for him that wanteth understanding, she saith to him, Come, eat of my bread, and drink of the wine which I have mingled. Forsake the foolish, and live; and go in the way of understanding (Prov. 9:1-6).

The text in Proverbs 9:1-6 could not be more of a contrast in scope than what we found in Proverbs 23:29-35 above. As we clearly observed, Solomon pictures the *yayin* as the bite of a dangerous cobra, whose end is swift and death follows. The consequences of ignoring his admonition are fatal. He demands that the reader *look not on the* yayin, for the hypnotizing powers of the snake's bottle will deceive you and in the end kill you.

Its redness . . . the sparkle of its eye in the cup . . . the fizz of curiosity is only for the fool. Its mocking scoff tricks by its outward beauty (20:1). No king drinks such poison, for it blinds the person to justice and clouds the person's sense of right (31:4). Yet the one who remains a walking corpse, condemned to death, tastes the adder's cup (31:6a), as too, can, in bitter irony, the one who lacks any hope (31:6b).

In Proverbs 9:1-6, however, exists the most obvious distinction. *Yayin* is detrimental to Wisdom's feast, which offers spiritual nourishment to its guests. Solomon says about *yayin look not!* But in this passage *yayin* is Wisdom's gift to life — insight and skill to live. In Proverbs 23 Solomon does not limit *yayin's* use; rather he counsels its firm avoidance, its plain abstinence. Here Solomon still does not limit *yayin's* use. In fact, he begs those at the table to partake: *Come, eat . . . drink of the yayin . . . and live . . . go in . . . understanding.* This is an open invitation to indulge!

Nor in Proverbs 9 does Wisdom offer her *yayin* to the wise, nor to the discerning or mature or even the self-controlled. Instead the table is set, the beasts are sacrificed, the bread is prepared, the *yayin* is poured, and the invitation to the simple — the one who lacks sense — is to enjoy. *Forsake your folly and live, And proceed in the way of understanding* (NASB). The folly is found away from the feast — the drink [*yayin, wine*]. Understanding is from [*yayin, wine*].

Solomon makes clear the distinction between *yayin* that is intoxicating, warned against, and from which to abstain (Prov. 23:29-35) and *yayin* that is encouraged to freely imbibe without the least concern for control (Prov. 9:1-6). Because this passage obviously is metaphoric in nature, some may sense that one must conclude *yayin* [wine] to be considered metaphoric as well, therefore draining out the force of the distinction. The difficulty is, if *yayin* [wine] is only of one kind—that is, intoxicating—what possible message could Solomon be communicating about both God, Whose wisdom is here portrayed, and *yayin* [wine] itself?

The clear indication is indulgence in feasting and drinking *yayin* [wine]. Teachout makes perfect sense as he counters the metaphoric sense objection. He concludes that such does not lessen the inconsistency that would still exist. Why? First, the one to whom the message was addressed is the naïve person who would be least likely to understand a subtle distinction between *yayin* [wine] as a dangerous deceiver (20:1) and *yayin* [wine] as a spiritual metaphor. Also, to picture God taking a harmful beverage—a beverage consistently portrayed elsewhere in Proverbs as suspiciously deviant and destructive and making it a symbol for beneficial spiritual truth—is questionable at best. Teachout concludes: "Since God has not considered it profitable to use this dubious procedure elsewhere in Scripture it is questionable, (at best) theologically, to champion such an understanding here."

Only those who insist on laying a film onto the text, assuming that *yayin* [wine] is singularly intoxicating, must look for alternate understanding. If we would but look at the text and allow the contextual content itself to inform us, we would easily conclude that the *yayin* [wine] in Proverbs 9:1-6 bears no resemblance to the intoxicating poisons in Proverbs 20 and 23.

Other passages in Proverbs

In this section we'll offer a brief commentary on some of the other passages found in Proverbs. Our goal is not to be exhaustive by any means. Rather we'll point out that many "wine" passages found in Scripture may be understood as consistently and helpfully bearing full support for total abstinence.

Proverbs 3:10: *So shall thy barns be filled with plenty, and thy presses shall burst out with new wine.* The blanket promise for the blessings of God cannot be ripped from condition in verse nine, which calls for "honoring the Lord" above everything else. And, such honor is to begin with the *firstfruits* of harvest. The term translated *wine* is *tirosh*, a less-prominent word but nonetheless important. Scholars debate whether the term *tirosh* always means *new wine*, as is seen in the translation above. Earlier lexicographers translated the term always as "fresh" and consequently unfermented. Later studies, however, question this conclusion. Reynolds makes a solid case that *tirosh* is used in the Old Testament synonymously with *yayin* and thus builds on the premise of later linguistics (Reynolds, 2003). Only the context, then, can determine whether *tirosh* is alcoholic wine or non-alcoholic wine. The promise that God gives to the faithful worshiper in this verse indicates the *presses* or "vats" where the grapes are processed will *burst* and overflow with the fresh sustenance God provides. Hence, the abundant wine is indicative of the abundant crop God bestows—heaven's harvest graciously given. No reason exists to suspect the wine in this verse is intoxicating wine.

Proverbs 4:17: *For they eat the bread of wickedness, and drink the wine of violence.* The point of this verse centers on the journey of the wicked man's lifestyle. Apparently the dishonest gain is procured through unlawful means, dubbed *wickedness*. Even the wicked man's bread and wine is secured at the high price of violence and crime—crimes from which the wicked receives the sadistic satisfaction of these pleasures fulfilled. The Bible is no stranger to the figurative expressions in which the effects of intoxicating wine are transposed to other contexts. Many times the judgment God bestows on the rebellious is indicated by wine's intoxicating properties (Ps. 60:3; 75:8; Isa. 51:17, 20-22; Jer. 51:7). Hence *the wine of violence* clearly implies an intoxicating product.

Proverbs 20:1: *Wine is a mocker, strong drink is raging: and whosoever is deceived thereby is not wise.* Since we've dealt with this verse earlier, only a few words are in order. First, we must insist that the description that this verse gives is about wine itself, not the one who drinks it. The *mocker* is *yayin*. Second, not one word implies that the one who is deceived has breached the so-called "rule of moderation." Abuse language is absent. As we saw earlier, the one who is *not wise* is the one who is not righteous or who is unholy.

Proverbs 31:4-7: *It is not for kings, O Lemuel, it is not for kings to drink wine; nor for princes strong drink: Lest they drink, and forget the law, and pervert the judgment of any of the afflicted. Give strong drink unto him that is ready to perish, and wine unto those that be of heavy hearts. Let him drink, and forget his poverty, and remember his misery no more.* First, the term translated *wine* is *yayin*, which is accompanied subsequently by unmistakable descriptors pointing to the intoxicating beverage. Second, the *wine* is forbidden to be used by those in authority, lest God's law be forgotten or justice be perverted. Third, the language of abstinence is clearly revealed that does not hint of a moderate consuming of either wine or strong drink. Once again *using* intoxicants and not *abusing* intoxicants is sliced by Scripture's blade. Not that Scripture does not clearly condemn drunkenness (Prov. 23:20-21; 29-35; Job 12:25; Ps. 107:27; Deut. 21:20; Isa. 19:14; 28:1, 3; Jer. 13:13; Nah. 1:10; Rom. 13:13; Eph. 5:18). The Bible certainly does condemn drunkenness and does so with severe judgment.

Finally, many commentators identify as criminals condemned to die the paradoxical exhortation to give strong *wine* to those who *perish*. Furthermore, *wine* is offered to people with *heavy hearts*—perhaps the destitute, the helpless, and the hopeless. To suggest the proverb has the force of moral command is mistaken on two counts. First, assuming a moral command, the presumption that Jesus would have broken such command by refusing the intoxicant as He was on the cross is unthinkable. Second, to give intoxicants to helpless, hopeless, destitute people, offering, at best, an illusion of relief squares not with one iota of divine benevolence we find in the entire biblical revelation. A command to be not only cruel but also deceptive is entirely unreasonable to conclude from this proverb. A bubbling moral irony overflows from this text.

Think of it: the highest aristocrats are commanded to abstain from intoxicants, but the most helpless people in society are to indulge. Solomon, therefore, appears to suggest that wine's ultimate value resides in the intoxicated minds of criminals and hopeless alike whose life possesses no meaning.

Conclusion

In summarizing, as we journey our way through the Book of Proverbs, a definitive pattern surfaces. This pattern undeniably steers our understanding of *wine* toward the ethic of abstinence. In places *wine* is seen as a blessing from God indicative of the abundant harvest the vineyard produces (Prov. 3:10). Nevertheless the images revealed about intoxicating wine as *mocker* that rages, deceives, and leads to unholiness cannot be glibly ignored by reading into the clear judgments from God a vague, extrabiblical measure that focuses entirely on *abuse* of intoxicants when the Scripture itself focuses on the *use* of intoxicants and clearly calls for abstinence in an age of indulgence.

Part 3

Chapter 12

Cana's Wedding, Cana's Wine: Liberating Jesus as the Moderationist Model

Indisputably the nail most often driven to morally fasten the recreational consumption of intoxicating beverages into a solid ethical structure originates in the New Testament. The Founder of Christianity Himself, the Second Person of the Blessed Trinity, God in human flesh—Jesus Christ—becomes the moderationist model. His practice, they say, unmistakably included *consuming* intoxicating beverages Himself, and, in the text before us, actually *creating* intoxicating beverages for others to consume. The alleged practice of which they speak has a long, rich history no one can deny. Even Jesus' own contemporaries utter a similar observation: *The Son of man is come eating and drinking; and ye say, Behold a gluttonous man, and a winebibber, a friend of publicans and sinners!* (Luke 7:34).

About the accusation the enemies of Christ hurl, one New Testament scholar summed it up like this: "One particular of that accusation men have continued to repeat until this day. They have said, and they have not ceased to say, Jesus was a drinking man. His enemies have insisted upon it . . . Lovers of strong drink have affirmed it, that they might shelter themselves under the cover of his example . . . Others [have] frankly avowed that no defense is demanded, but that course as a moderate drinker is to be copied" (Field, 1883).

The miracle at Cana, along with a few other texts, we're told, convincingly demonstrate beyond reasonable doubt that Jesus' regular practice as the Bible records includes consumption of intoxicating beverages—so much so in fact, He is mistakenly dubbed a *drunkard*. Yet the unproven premise on which such an interpretation depends is the very premise under consideration here. G.I. Williamson, a notable advocate for the moderate consumption of intoxicating beverages, writes, "Though our Lord was accused of being *a gluttonous man and a drunkard* (Luke 7:34) they knew . . . one could lawfully eat without being a glutton and drink without being a drunkard. It would not offend them to hear that their Lord made wine for a wedding feast . . . They did not attempt to rewrite Scripture so as to make the word *wine* stand for grape juice . . ." (Williamson, 1999). Williamson tacitly assumes the miraculous wine Jesus creates to be intoxicating wine. Even more, however, to interpret the wine Jesus both consumes and creates as non-intoxicating wine apparently is a conspiracy—an attempt to *rewrite Scripture*. One recalls the "tortured exegesis" that sacrifices the "integrity" and "sufficiency" of Scripture alleged by the seminary professor we recorded earlier. The eminent John Owen did not think so. In his commentary on John's gospel Owen concluded the wine Jesus creates is the "pure juice of the grape" and therefore is "wholly free from the alcoholic stimulant."

What should not be lost is the fact that all parties agree, at least in part, with the expressed focus of the moderationists. That is, the *locus classicus* in dealing with what constitutes moral behavior cannot be other than that rooted in the personal behavior of the Lord Jesus. If Jesus was a social consumer of intoxicating drink, how could anyone seriously object to such a behavioral practice? If one's moral construct insists that recreationally consuming intoxicants is wrongful, God-dishonoring behavior, and supposing the Son of God Himself embodies such questionable behavior, an unpleasant, impossible dilemma follows for the advocate of abstinence.

On the other hand, to insist without evidence, as those who lobby for the recreational, moderate consumption of alcoholic beverages, on making our Savior, the Lord Jesus Christ, the pristine example of moderate imbibing, and to do so in the face of contrary evidence we intend on showing, an even greater dilemma follows, since such insistence borders on smearing both the name and character of our Savior.

No one to date better captures this dilemma than does New Testament scholar Leon C. Field. In 1882 Field penned a series of articles for *The Methodist Quarterly* collected and published the following year by Phillips & Hunt, New York, under one title. So influential within the scholarly community was this volume, the journal of *The New Hampshire Annual Conference* characterized Field's work as "a masterly and exhaustive argument on the subject, which has never been overthrown and which has elicited favorable comment by the best minds on both sides of the Atlantic" (Tait, N/D).

Field argues that if advocates for moderate alcohol use are correct in asserting that Jesus Himself, in the Scriptures, moderately consumes intoxicants strictly for pleasure, such would "prove exceedingly damaging, if not utterly fatal, to the claims of total abstinence." "Christ must be determinative in this matter," he writes. He acknowledges, "If their premises are correct their conclusion is inevitable."

Further along Field makes even clearer that the moral example of Jesus is non-negotiable in understanding the use of intoxicating drugs. With incontrovertible logic Field reasons:

"If [Jesus] drank alcoholic beverages we may do the same. Not that we *must,* but we *may.* There can be no obligation to abstain which he would not have recognized and enforced by his own example. If he indulged, indulgence is innocent . . . If he has sanctioned the habit of wine-drinking by his practice, that fact must outweigh every other in a controversy upon the subject. If the charge which is brought against him of being a wine-bibber be sustained, then we have no invulnerable argument with which to urge the duty of total abstinence . . . Every thing that is vital to this great issue is determined by Christ's position upon the question" (Field, 1883).

As we briefly examine the miracle at Cana, considerations concerning *wine* in other passages may arise, especially as they apply to Jesus' view, but for the most part, other texts will be considered in appendices. My primary thrust is to liberate Jesus from the clutches of moderationists who insist our Savior undeniably serves as the supreme example of why they or others may socially, leisurely, and pleasurably consume intoxicating beverages with the full blessing of God on them. In the end, as Professor Field suggests, all that is vital to this issue ultimately is determined by Christ's position on the question.

The miracle at Cana: *oinos*

When the ruler of the feast had tasted the water that was made wine, and knew not whence it was: (but the servants which drew the water knew;) the governor of the feast called the bridegroom, And saith unto him, Every man at the beginning doth set forth good wine; and when men have well drunk, then that which is worse: but thou hast kept the good wine until now. This beginning of miracles did Jesus in Cana of Galilee, and manifested forth his glory; and his disciples believed on him (John 2:9-11).

John's particularity as a gospel writer needs no emphasis. The literary ingenuity the Holy Spirit gave him and through which He infallibly guided him as he penned the Word of God remains unsurpassed. No sooner than one's eyes latch on to the very first words of the gospel does our mind know and our heart predict One greater than Jonah is here: *In the beginning was the Word, and the Word was with God, and the Word was*

God. The same was in the beginning with God. All things were made by him; and without him was not any thing made that was made (John 1:1-3).

Curiosity may be raised as to why we begin a study on John chapter two with John chapter one. Who Jesus is and proclaims to be in John 1 gives a necessary background for properly understanding Jesus' first miracle at Cana in John 2. In the first chapter seven characteristics are made of Jesus by different witnesses (Gordon, 1944). In John 1 He is revealed as both *light of men* and *Lamb of God* (vv. 4, 29). Jesus is the *son of Joseph* and the *Son of man* (vv. 45, 51), etc. For our purposes Nathanael's eureka moment is superb and stands as the pinnacle of the narrative: *thou art the Son of God* (v. 49). Such inspiring testimony reflects perfectly with John's opening statement: *the Word was God . . . All things were made by him . . . And the Word was made flesh, and dwelt among us . . .* (vv. 1, 3, 14).

Let's keep such in mind as we move on now to Cana and Christ's first miracle. Mary, the mother of Jesus, has been invited to a wedding, presumably as was the entire family. No mention is made of Joseph, whom many believe probably has died by this time in Jesus' life. Weddings could last more than several days and demand lots of energy as well as food and drink. Accordingly, the wine runs out; this occasions Mary to approach Jesus inquiring what He will do. After His conversation with her He instructs the servants to fill with water six large stone pots.

Undoubtedly the pots serve a ritualistic purpose, used for the guests and in total hold between 120 and 180 gallons of liquid (Morris L., 1971). Once the jars are filled, Jesus instructs the servants to draw from the jars and give to the wedding host. Overcome with delight the host proclaims the water that Jesus makes into wine the best: *Every man at the beginning doth set forth good wine; and when men have well drunk, then that which is worse: but thou hast kept the good wine until now* (v. 10). The headmaster was "astounded by the high quality of the wine since generally a poorer quality was served once the taste of the guests became dulled" (Tenney, 1981).

The Apostle John concludes this miracle or *sign* as the first sign in John's Gospel that *manifested forth his glory* (v. 10). And, while this sign surely deserves more devoted attention than a raw look at its incidental properties—the transformation of water to wine—we must content ourselves presently with such.

The Greek term *oinos* translated *wine* is used six times in the above passage. Invariably it is translated *wine* in all English Bibles. At least five other terms are translated *wine* in the New Testament: *gleukos* (Acts 2:13 only); *lenos* (used five times, only one of which is not in Revelation); *oxos* (used six times, all referring to the wine Jesus is offered on the cross); *paroinos*: (used only twice exclusively of an overseer's qualifications); *hypolenion*: (only in Mark 12:1 for the lower wine vat). Nevertheless *oinos* remains the dominant word the apostolic authors use.

At the outset we wonder whether the term *oinos* indicates intoxicating beverage each and every time it is used in the New Testament, similarly to the way we queried whether the Hebrew term *yayin* was indicative of intoxicating wine each and every time the term is used in the Old Testament. We learned *yayin* is a generic term and could be used for both freshly-squeezed grape juice as well as exceedingly strong intoxicating drink. The context made much of the difference in the way we understood the term. Thus we ask, is *oinos* generic as well? Many today argue that every time we find the term *wine* [*oinos*] in the New Testament, invariably the wine is intoxicating. Indeed moderationists insist that Jesus supports the consumption of alcoholic beverages and do so on the assumption that all wine [*oinos*] is intoxicating wine, including the wine [*oinos*] He miraculously makes from water.

Nonetheless a substantial amount of impressive scholarship in this area appears to be overlooked; that research at least on the surface definitively questions the moderationist's premise. The fact is, the Greek term *oinos*, if we are to believe renowned scholars of an earlier era, is decidedly generic similarly to the way the Hebrew term *yayin* is.

For example Field boldly asserts "[*Oinos*] occurs thirty-two times, outnumbering all the other terms in use four to one. It has the same generic sense in the New Testament that it has in classic usage, and that *yayin* has in the Hebrew" (Field, 1883). Furthermore, the world-renowned 19th-century Andover scholar Moses Stuart writes: "In the New Testament we have *oinos*, which corresponds exactly with the Hebrew *yayin*." Field continues, arguing that *oinos* actually possesses a wider range of meaning than *yayin*. Indeed, as Field analyzes the usage, he concludes *oinos* comprehends "new wine" (*oinos neos*, Mt. 9:17 and Mark 2:22), "sweet wine" (*gleukos* Acts 2:13), and "sour wine" (*oxus* Mark 15:23).

In addition Robert Teachout, in his more recent unpublished doctoral dissertation, an exhaustive study of wine in the Old Testament, concludes similarly with both Field and Stuart. After offering an impressive amount of linguistic evidence pertaining to the study of Hebrew (*yayin*), Latin (*vinum*), and classical Greek (*oinos*) usages of our English term *wine*, Teachout writes: "These sources from the Greco-Roman world give unmistakable evidence that Greek *oinos* and Latin *vinum* can refer to fresh juice as well as to fermented wine . . . It is well to note that the New Testament does retain the meaning of fresh juice for *oinos*" (Teachout, 1979).

One linguistic thread scholars trace to conclude that *oinos* is generic concerns its saturation in the **Septuagint** (LXX), the Greek translation of the Old Testament commonly used by both the church at large and the New Testament authors. The two major words in the Old Testament translated as *wine* are *tirosh* and *yayin*. Teachout found that in those passages in which *tirosh* is used in the Hebrew text—38 times in all—with only two exceptions the translators of the LXX used the Greek term *oinos*. The term *yayin* is also translated by the Greek word *oinos*. Hence, since both *yayin* and *tirosh* are generic and can be both intoxicating and unintoxicating, *oinos* appears also to be a generic term as well.

Add to the evidence the LXX gives, the classical etymology of *oinos* clearly revealing *oinos* as a generic term (see Appendices). One can understand why scholars are reluctant to read *wine* in the New Testament invariably as intoxicating wine. For example Aristotle and Nicander both use *oinos* [*wine*] for an unintoxicating beverage. Thus, in light of this, one should remain reluctant to embrace the premise that whenever the New Testament speaks of *wine* [*oinos*], the New Testament speaks of intoxicating wine. While *wine* [*oinos*] in the New Testament is every bit as intoxicating and potent as wine in the Old Testament (Gen. 9:21; Eph. 5:18), the evidence seems clear that *wine* [*oinos*] may lack intoxicants. And, the absence or presence of intoxicants are detected, if possible, from the context of the biblical passage itself.

Jesus created wine

We've concluded *wine* [*oinos*] may or may not have been intoxicating. From the term itself we can offer no conclusion. Based on linguistics *alone* the moderationist may be right: Jesus creates intoxicating wine. No less so, based on linguistics *alone*, abstinence adherents very well may be right: Jesus does not make intoxicating wine. Thus those of us who argue for abstinence may not, at least at this point, claim victory. As Field argues, since *oinos* is the substance Jesus creates, and *oinos* is a generic term offering us no intimation as to its nature, "we must decide by internal evidence and moral likelihood whether the wine was alcoholic or the contrary."

A fair warning to those who embrace consuming intoxicating beverages for pleasurable purposes: to base one's moral principle on the alleged character and behavior of Jesus when no indisputable biblical evidence to substantiate it exists is ethically unworthy.

The meaning of *oinos* in John 2 is significant but does not stand alone as the reason to reject the assertion that Jesus created intoxicating wine. The Cana miracle, as John says, *manifested his glory*. Are we to believe the Son of God *manifested his glory* by sprucing up a wedding party because it ran out of wine? Was the Lord's focus on social success—making sure that an earthly festival had plenty of supplies so people could have a good time? Surely *manifested his glory* connects at a higher level—a greater Messianic dimension than securing free wine. What would be the higher purpose?

In the biblical account Jesus creates wine as an announcement of Himself as both Creator and Redeemer. He is fulfilling prophecy of His incarnation and approaching death. Recall John begins his gospel stating the Word was God and the Word became flesh and dwelt among us. The Word incarnate is the Word concerning whom John records, *All things were made by him; and without him was not any thing made that was made* (v. 3). The Second Person of the Trinity, the Eternal Word made flesh, the Creator sits with the people in Cana. God is in town!

After Jesus leaves Cana, we find a similar announcement He makes, for He goes to the temple and demonstrates He is Lord of the temple (2:12-22). He rebukes the wretched defilement He finds and shows the bankruptcy temple worship has become. Consequently the temple is cleansed; a new order—a New Covenant begins.

When we think then of Jesus creating wine—manifesting His glory—and His disciples believing on Him as a result (v. 11), we think of him as Creator and Redeemer. K.T. Cooper writes, "The [Cana miracle] is a sign, and in John every sign points beyond itself to an aspect of the person and work of the Messiah. The restoration of sight to the blind man points to

Jesus as the light of the world; the multiplication of the loaves points to Jesus the bread of life; the raising of Lazarus points to Jesus the resurrection and the life" (Cooper, 1979).

If this is so, to imagine Christ making wine any less than the freshest, purest liquid sustenance is inconceivable. Those who insist to the contrary—asserting the wine Jesus makes is intoxicating—do so against all reason. For the fact is *fermented* wine is *decayed* wine; that is *wine by its chemical makeup is impure.* During fermentation, when the sugar of the grape is exposed to microorganisms, what is produced is gas and alcohol, neither compound of which is inherent to the grape. Alcohol is foreign. Alcohol is an invader. The natural sugar of the grape God creates is absent from fermented wine. Thus, to be fermented wine on all accounts is to be inferior wine. As Creator, Christ Jesus the Lord makes water into the freshest, most delightful grape juice imaginable.

Water into grape juice

Some may wonder whether such an interpretation is a novelty—a quaint rationalizing of the text because the standard interpretation that Jesus made intoxicating wine is both offensive and inconvenient to the abstinence advocate. Such is not the case, I assure. The fact is that the view that sees Jesus creating fresh, wholesome grape juice has a long, rich interpretive heritage.

For example Saint Augustine in his homily on this passage reads, "He who made wine on that day at the marriage feast . . . the self-same does this every year in vines . . . in like manner also is what the clouds pour forth changed into wine by the doing of the same Lord . . . it happens every year" (Augustine, 2000). Chrysostom held similar views (Chrysostom, 2000).

R.C. Trench, in his classic on Jesus' miracles, concludes, "He who does every year prepare the wine in the grape, causing it to drink up and expand with the moisture of earth and heaven, to take this up into itself, and transmute into its own nobler juices, did now gather together all those his slower processes into the act of a single moment, and accomplish in an instant what ordinarily he does not accomplish but in many months" (Trench, 1850).

Many more witnesses could be added to the above, demonstrating the rich interpretative heritage within which abstinence advocates remain. In short, abstentionists have employed neither a hermeneutical novelty nor "tortured exegesis" to bolster their position. What we hold, we hold firmly, decidedly on Scripture.

Better advice cannot be found than the advice offered from Albert Barnes on this passage of Scripture. After affirming what we've here argued, Barnes charges we have no right to read our contemporary understanding of modern wines back into the Bible. Barnes then makes this solemn warning all students of Scripture should appreciate:

"No man should adduce THIS instance in favor of drinking wine unless he can prove that the wine made in the waterpots of Cana was JUST LIKE the wine which he proposes to drink. The Saviour's example may be always pleaded JUST AS IT WAS; but it is a matter of obvious and simple justice that we should find out exactly what the example was before we plead it (caps original) (Barnes, Barnes Notes on the Bible, V. 12 John, 2000).

Some argue that the description the master of the banquet gives about the wine Christ provides as *the good wine* means a high-quality alcoholic wine. However, to assume *good* wine to be *alcoholic* wine not only begs the question, it also reads our modern ways of evaluating the quality of wine back into the first century. Why would good wine necessarily be intoxicating? In fact just the opposite is true. Jacobus writes, "those [wines] were esteemed the best wines which were least strong." Stuart asserts of the unfermented wines in the first century, "it was regarded as if a higher and better quality than any other." Albert Barnes, in his commentary on John's gospel about alcoholic strength as a test of *good* wine, writes: "We use the phrase to denote that it is good in proportion to its strength, and its power to intoxicate. But no such sense is to be attached to the word here." Barnes further notes that Greek writers frequently mention that *good* wine was harmless or "innocent". This means those wines did not intoxicate.

Pliny, the first-century Roman historian, says "wines are most beneficial when all their potency has been removed by the strainer." Plutarch similarly asserts wine is more pleasant to drink when it neither "inflames the brain nor infests the mind or passions" (Bacchiocchi, 2004). Hence the wine Christ creates is *good* not because it is strong or contains a high concentrate of alcohol. Instead Christ's wine is *good* because of its *purity*.

Therefore, when we examine the biblical record of Christ's first miracle at Cana, we find a marvelous announcement that the Word through Whom all things are made has become flesh and dwells among human beings. He *manifested his glory* by creating wine. And the wine He creates remains unlike any wine before drunk. It is a pure, unadulterated sweet-water from the grape—refreshing to the taste and satisfying to the soul. Unlike the manufactured wines Israel produced through ancient means of crushing grapes and bagging juice, this wine is straight from God. Similar to the fresh bread Jesus makes, offering to the people the true bread from heaven (John 6:1-31), Christ makes the fresh new wine indicative of the New Covenant He offers the sinful world.

Appendices

Annotated Texts

In this appendix are several biblical texts from both Old and New Testaments with which we did not deal in the body of the book. I've included annotations on each text to give the reader a sense of interpretation consistent with abstinence that we've offered. The list by no means is exhaustive. However, the texts chosen represent many of the significant Bible passages about wine.

Numbers 6:3-4

He shall separate himself from wine [yayin] and strong drink [shekar], and shall drink no vinegar of wine [yayin], or vinegar of strong drink [shekar], neither shall he drink any liquor of grapes, nor eat moist grapes, or dried. All the days of his separation shall he eat nothing that is made of the vine tree, from the kernels even to the husk.

This text concerns the law of the Nazarite. Thus these are special instructions given to those who are set aside for special purposes. The most famous Old Testament Nazarite was Samson (Judg. 13); the most famous New Testament Nazarite was John the Baptist (Luke 1:13-15). What's of interest in these verses are the two terms for wine: *yayin* and *shekar*. *Yayin* is the most frequently used word translated *wine* in the Old Testament. Earlier we learned the generic nature of *yayin* —that is, *yayin* could be either an intoxicating or non-intoxicating grape product.

What of the term *shekar* translated into the English Bible as *strong drink*? Because the English translation has *strong* modifying *drink*, to assume *shekar* is an intensified intoxicant remains tempting. The assumption is questionable, however. For example, Moses Stuart argues that *shekar* is a generic term used in the very same sense as is *yayin*. He further argues that *shekar* was actually less strong than was ordinary wine since it probably originated from dates, millets, etc. Teachout similarly argues *shekar* could be freshly-squeezed fruit juices as well. Even more interesting is the second prohibition to the Nazarite: he was not to partake of the *vinegar* of either *yayin* or *shekar*. Stuart insists, "Manifestly the idea conveyed by our translation here is wrong. The vinegar of wine and the vinegar of strong drink, (as our version has it,) were no more employed as drinks by the Hebrews than vinegar of cider or wine is used for drink by us." Instead he argues that the root word for *vinegar* has to do with *leaven* and therefore *ferment*. He concludes that the expressions mean "fermented wine and fermented *shekar*." If Stuart is correct, such insight goes a long way in clearing up several passages of Scripture.

Deuteronomy 14:23, 26

And thou shalt eat before the Lord thy God, in the place which he shall choose to place his name there, the tithe of thy corn, of thy wine [tirosh], and of thine oil, and the firstlings of thy herds and of thy flocks; that thou mayest learn to fear the Lord thy God always . . . And thou shalt bestow that money for whatsoever thy soul lusteth after, for oxen, or for sheep, or for wine [yayin], or for strong drink [shekar], or for whatsoever thy soul desireth: and thou shalt eat there before the Lord thy God, and thou shalt rejoice, thou, and thine household.

The instructions to Israel in this passage pertain to the annual harvest festival offerings. The worshipers are to bring tithes of the harvest blessings God bestows on them. For those traveling a long way special instructions are given to accommodate for the trip. The *delayed tithe,* as some call it, is the number-one text advocates for drink use to demonstrate that God approves of both wine and strong drink. Kenneth Gentry asserts "the divine sanction is unmistakable."

Does the text above prove moderate consumption of alcoholic beverages is morally acceptable to God? The answer must be *no*. First, the passage reveals nothing about drinking alcoholic beverages for pleasure. The text does say the worshipers can purchase whatever they desire. But the text does not say the worshipers are to drink whatever they desire. Furthermore, the text also says that the people can buy oxen or sheep. Yet it doesn't mention what is to be done to the sheep or oxen and makes no sense to assume the people will consume them raw. In the same sense both *yayin* and *shekar* are likely heavily diluted, whether intoxicating or not. Do those who advocate intoxicating drink also advocate diluting the intoxicating drink?

Second, because overwhelming evidence exists that *yayin* is generic, no reason compels us to believe *yayin* in this passage is necessarily intoxicating. In fact, because intoxicants are banned from priestly participation during temple worship, the likelihood worshipers would be allowed to imbibe intoxicants is unreasonable. Third, if Stuart is correct and *shekar* is generic similarly to *yayin*, the case is closed. No definitive sanction for alcohol consumption in these verses is forthcoming. Admittedly diversity remains on the meaning of *shekar* even among commentators who fully embrace biblical abstinence. For example Adam Clarke says of *shekar*, the word "signifies any kind of *fermented* liquors." Nevertheless, since nothing conclusive may be drawn concerning *shekar*, the fact that this passage serves as evidence for moderate consumption of alcoholic beverages remains questionable.

Ecclesiastes 9:7

Go thy way, eat thy bread with joy, and drink thy wine[yayin] with a merry heart; for God now accepteth thy works.

First, intoxication is not mentioned in this passage. One cannot assume because the text says *a merry heart*, it therefore means intoxication. The term translated *merry* is used more than 500 times in the Old Testament, the first time of which is used of God (Gen. 1:4). *Merry* has dozens of nuances, none of which is specifically related to intoxication. Incidentally, are those who insist *merry* is an exhilarating physiological effect of wine prepared to accept *joy* as an exhilarating physiological effect of bread? Lees concludes, "Those who conclude that the wine approved in Scripture must have been intoxicating because said to give pleasure [sic], are refuted by this very passage, in which the eating of 'bread' is associated with 'gladness'—*simkhah*—a term descriptive of the highest delight."

Second, the primary thrust seems to be gratitude for God's benefits. Even so, given Ecclesiastes' tendency for cynicism apart from God, this verse very well could possess a cynical outlook on human existence.

Isaiah 25:6

And in this mountain shall the Lord of hosts make unto all people a feast of fat things, a feast of wines[shemer] on the lees, of fat things full of marrow, of wines[shemer] on the lees well refined.

Lees believes the *shemer* refers to preserves, a thick paste made from the cooked and aged grapes. Clarke quotes Sir Edward Barry, arguing "wine on the lees" was an ancient method making the wine stronger but not necessarily more potent with intoxicants. In other words the goal was for robust flavor, not to give it more "kick." Reynolds thinks the Jewish translation of the Old Testament—The Tanakh—may be closest, as it translates *wines on the lees* as *choice wines*. Whatever the case the Hebrew is apparently much too vague to possess any degree of certainty about this passage. Thus to employ it as a text to show imbibing alcohol as morally acceptable remains specious at best.

Luke 7:33-34

For John the Baptist came neither eating bread nor drinking wine [oinos]; and ye say, He hath a devil. The Son of man is come eating and drinking; and ye say, Behold a gluttonous man, and a winebibber[oinopotes], a friend of publicans and sinners! (cp. Mt. 11:19).

Many attempt to use this passage to argue that Jesus drinks intoxicating beverages. First, one must recall precisely who makes this charge against Jesus. His enemies! When do his enemies ever care about accuracy? They say John the Baptist is demonized. Should we believe them? Second, whether *oinos* is an intoxicating beverage in this passage is entirely unclear. These verses prove nothing about the practices of Jesus about intoxicating beverages. Albert Barnes concludes, "As wine was a common article of beverage among the people, he drank it. It was the pure juice of the grape, and, for anything that can be proved, it was without fermentation . . ." (Barnes, Mt. 11).

Romans 14:21

It is good neither to eat flesh, nor to drink wine [oinos], nor any thing whereby thy brother stumbleth, or is offended, or is made weak.

Interestingly, British pastor and theologian Peter Masters, in his book *Should Christians Drink?*, concedes this verse to opponents of abstention. He writes, "Paul's words do not, when correctly interpreted, speak about setting a bad example." Instead he agrees with those who advocate moderate consumption of alcoholic beverages that when Paul speaks of the weaker brother, he is not thinking of a person who might be led to take a drink and so potentially become an alcoholic. Rather Paul is concerned with the brother who is weak because he believes that if he eats or drinks certain things, he'd somehow be defiled and made unclean in God's sight. In other words Paul is concerned with superstitious fetishes that apparently are prevalent in Rome. Nonetheless Masters argues conceding this verse does not weaken the believer's responsibility to live worthy examples for others to follow. He rightly asks, "What about all the other texts which command believers not to set a potentially dangerous example to their fellows?" (2 Cor. 6:3-4; 11:29).

Ephesians 5:18

And be not drunk [methusko] with wine [oinos], wherein is excess; but be filled with the Spirit.

This may be the most often-cited text in the New Testament not only to demonstrate *oinos* to be an intoxicating beverage but also to imply the Bible's focus is on "excess" in drinking, not drinking itself. First, no one disputes whether *oinos* was an intoxicating beverage in the first century. The question is whether *oinos* was *exclusively* an intoxicating beverage. And, from classical Greek usage as well as the usage of *oinos* in the LXX, abstentionists seem to have the upper ground. Stuart, Field, Samson, Maguire, Nott, Teachout, Barnes, Clarke, Lees, and a host of other eminent scholars insist on the generic nature of *oinos*.

Second, moderation is not so much as mentioned in this verse. Two contradictory extremes are mentioned: drunk with wine and filled with the Spirit, with the implication that if one state exists, the other cannot. Cleon Rogers writes an interesting paper about the Dionysian background of Ephesus and connecting Ephesians 5:18 to the religious cult so prominent in Ephesus (Rogers, 1979).

Connected with the cult festivals was the wild, frenzied dancing and uncontrolled ravings, all under the spell of excessive wine drinking. Rogers sees a parallel between being *filled with the Spirit* and being "filled with Bacchus." He reasons, "If the filling of the Spirit has to do with a supernatural infilling of the Spirit of the living God, it would only be logical to suppose that the '*drunk with wine*' could have a supernatural implication. The significance would then be a contrast with the filling of the 'spirit' of Bacchus through wine and the filling of the true and living God by His Spirit." His case is fascinating and cannot be easily dismissed. Even so, once again moderationists cannot claim with certainty one of their favorite proof-texts to substantiate moderate consumption of intoxicating beverages.

Colossians 2:16-17

Let no man therefore judge you in meat, or in drink, or in respect of an holyday, or of the new moon, or of the sabbath days: Which are a shadow of things to come; but the body is of Christ.

These verses often are used by advocates for moderate consumption of alcoholic beverages to rebuke abstentionists from judging what other believers are eating and/or drinking. The apostle plainly says those things are a *shadow of things to come.* Christ puts an end to the ceremonial legalism of Old Testament law. In response Paul is dealing with legalistic Judaizers who attempt to impose Old Testament law on New Testament Christians—especially on Gentile Christians. Therefore, the meat, drink, holyday, etc., specifically pertain to the ceremonial law. However, as Stephen Reynolds points out, "the dietary laws are abolished for Christians, but the moral law is still in full force." Proverbs 23:31, for example, gives a moral prohibition about intoxicating substances, not a ceremonial prohibition. Therefore, these verses present no challenge to abstentionists.

Pastoral letters

Not given to wine [paroinos] (1 Tim. 3:3); *not given to much wine[oinos]* (1 Tim. 3:8); *use a little wine[oinos] for thy stomach's sake and thine often infirmities* (1 Tim. 5:23); *not given to wine [oinos]* (Titus 1:7); *not given to much wine[oinos]* (Titus 2:3).

First, Paul's advice to Timothy to *use a little wine* for his stomach easily may be dismissed as warrant for moderate consumption of alcoholic beverages. No one disputes the medicinal usage of intoxicants. Paul says *use* it; he does not say drink it for pleasure. Second, once again the uncertainty about the wine Paul prescribes cannot be overlooked. Not only is *oinos* a generic term for *wine*, but also ancient testimony exists that explicitly affirms non-intoxicating wine was used for stomach problems. Therefore, we cannot say for certain what kind of wine Paul prescribes. As for Paul's instructions to bishops (1 Tim. 3:3; Titus 1:7), the term *paroinos* literally means *beside* or *alongside wine*. John MacArthur writes, "more than a mere prohibition against drunkenness . . . an Elder must not have a reputation for drinking" (MacArthur). The English Standard Bible interestingly reduces Paul's phrase to a "mere prohibition" of drunkenness. Given the general negativity toward intoxicants and Paul's instructions to not be *alongside* wine, we are better off taking the injunctions to bishops as to appealing to abstinence. Finally, many take the qualifier *much* when Paul speaks to deacons as an implicit sanction to imbibe. However, such appears to be grasping for any evidence whatsoever to substantiate a flawed case. Paul's commanding deacons to abstain from *much* wine says nothing at all for or against abstaining from moderate drinking. As Bacchiocchi incisively suggests, what is forbidden in much does not automatically imply permitted in little (Bacchiocchi, 2004). Suppose someone questioned the appropriateness of a married man often visiting a single woman with "He surely does spend entirely too much time over there." Would we properly deduce that while too much time is inappropriate, a little time would not be? When the apostle speaks of not addicted to *much wine*, he's not softening the leadership requirement. Rather he's speaking a bit more loosely, that's all.

Glossary

Absolute: a concept that is perfect and unchangeable, not modified by culture or circumstances. A *moral absolute* is a principle that is true for all people in all places at all times.

Abstinence: a self-denial of desires to indulge; as used in this volume, one who refrains from consuming intoxicating substances for pleasurable purposes.

Adiaphora: this Greek term is used in the ethical sense of matters outside moral concern. For example moral principle is unconcerned with whether one prefers chocolate or vanilla ice cream.

Alcopops: alcoholic beverages sweetened with various fruit juices and packaged in colorful, glitzy wrapping marketed especially for the young drinker.

Antinomianism: the term literally means "against law" and normally is used in the sense of freedom from the moral law in the gospel dispensation.

Conservative Resurgence: officially launched in 1979, a concerned group of grassroots Southern Baptists began to deal with creeping liberalism in the Southern Baptist Convention. The key issue concerned the inerrancy of Scripture. Through concerted effort and tireless service conservative Southern Baptists regained leadership and steered the convention back to its biblical rootedness.

Deontological: this term concerns one's duty to be moral and stresses obligation to principle rather than result-centered ethics (see teleological).

Ecclesiology: the study of the church; its structure, organization, and purpose according to the New Testament.

Ethyl alcohol: the chemical composition for ethyl alcohol, otherwise known as alcohol, is C_2H_5OH. The formula indicates composure of two carbons, one oxygen, and six atoms of hydrogen.

Ethical relativism: the moral premise that all behavior depends on culture, time, and progress. Relativism contrasts with absolutism (see previous page).

Hedonism: the view that pleasure and the fulfillment of it is the highest value of life and should be sought for its own sake alone.

Inerrancy: the view of biblical inspiration that insists on accepting what the Bible says about itself. Consequently the end result is that the Bible is truth without any mixture of error whatsoever.

Liberal: depending on the historical era, the term *liberal* may be used to refer to any position that denies the Bible's complete, absolute authority for faith and practice.

Libertine: not to be confused with the term *liberal* above, *libertine* suggests freedom of human action, a lack of restraint. In ethics the term could be seen synonymous with *antinomianism* (see above).

Moderation: the view that insists consumption of intoxicating substances is morally acceptable when consumed in reasonable amounts. Though no definition appears available from moderationists to define what "reasonable amounts" are, perhaps we best view "reasonable amounts" as relative and therefore just short of intoxication.

Moderate: the term is used in theological circles to be a "middle way" between Fundamentalism and Liberalism.

Moral Construct: in this volume, while moral construct has been used in singular sense—that is, equivalent to a moral rule or guideline—overall moral construct points to a broader idea that encompasses an entire ethical view.

Prohibition Era: a period in the United States from 1919 to 1933 in which the manufacture, distribution, and sale of intoxicating beverages was banned nationally as mandated by constitutional law.

Postmodern: a complicated term to define; my use of this term is usually limited to the sense that depicts an outlook on reality as being less than rational. Postmodern thinking sees many "truths" all competing but no one truth determining. *Postmodern* is a denial of absolutes.

Recreational: specifically related to pleasure

Syllogisms: term often used in the discipline of logic referencing the way ideas relate and testing whether the ideas are contradictory. In ethics, moral reasoning many times takes the form of syllogisms and tests whether moral ideas are consistent.

Teleological: results-based ethics. The outcome is more important than is the rule. The outcome is the moral principle.

Temperance Movement: the movement in this country lasting for the entire 19th century leading to the federal prohibition of intoxicating beverages in 1919.

Utilitarianism: the idea that the right action is what brings the greatest good for the greatest number of people.

Viticulture: a branch of the science of horticulture, viticulture is the study of grapes.

Historical References

The following sources assist us in understanding wine as did the ancients. One clearly deduces from sources below that wine in antiquity was both fermented and unfermented, intoxicating and non-intoxicating:

Cato the Elder, the famous Roman historian: "According to this regulation, the hanging wine [*vinum*] ought to be sold. You are to leave the husks unwatered, and the dregs. A place shall be set apart for the wine [*vinum*], down to the first kalends of October; if you have not carried them clear off before, the proprietor shall do whatever he pleases with the wine [*vinum*]." The Latin *vinum* is equivalent to *oinos* in Greek. Here the hanging clusters of grapes are clearly referred as *hanging wine*, which is hardly to be confused with intoxicating drink.

Ovid, the Roman Poet: "And scarce the grapes contain the wine [*vinum*] within." Once again, the unprocessed juice in the grape is referred as wine.

Plautus, a Roman Playwright, living about two centuries before Christ signified *must* [Latin, for *grape juice*] as "both wine and sweet juice."

Aristotle: speaking of sweet wine, Aristotle writes "that sweet wine [*oinos*, the Greek term used throughout the New Testament for wine] would not intoxicate."

Nicander, the Greek Poet and physician of the second century B.C.: "And Cenus having squeezed the juice of the grapes, into hollow cups, called it wine (*oinos*)." Thus, from both Aristotle and Nicander we have evidence to assume that when *wine* is used in the New Testament, based on the way the term *oinos* was employed in classical Greek, for us to tacitly assume that *wine* always means intoxicating beverage remains unacceptable.

Horace, the famous Roman Poet at the time of Augustus Caesar: He tells his friend Mecaenas that he might drink "hundred glasses of this innocent Lesbian [possibly referring to the Greek island in the northeastern Aegean Sea]" without any danger to his head or senses. In the Delphian edition of Horace we are told that "Lesbian wine could injure no one" since it would neither "affect the head nor inflame the passions." Added is the statement that "there is no wine sweeter to drink than Lesbian; that it was like nectar, and more resembled ambrosia than wine; that it was perfectly harmless, and would not produce intoxication."

Athenaeus, a Greek rhetorician and grammarian: "Surrentine wine was fat and very weak." The description commonly indicates an impotent after-effect.

Pliny, a Roman historian and philosopher and contemporary of Jesus and the Apostles: "Surrentine wine does not affect the head." Furthermore, Pliny indicates a Spanish wine simply called "a wine which would not intoxicate."

Theophrastus, a Greek philosopher who succeeded Aristotle: he called wine that had been wine deprived of its strength *castratum* and therefore "moral wine." In other words this wine would not intoxicate.

Columella, a Roman writer and contemporary of Jesus Christ: speaking of the "weak wines" of Greece, he says, "Those small Greek wines, as the Mareotic, Thasian, Psythian, Sophortian, though they have a tolerable good taste, yet, in our climate, they yield but little wine, from the thinness of their clusters, and the smallness of their berries. Nevertheless, the black Inerticula (the sluggish vine), which some Greeks call Amethyston, may be placed, as it were, in the second tribe, because it both yields a good wine, and is harmless from which, also, it took its name because it is reckoned dull, and not to have spirit enough to affect the nerves, though it is not dull and flat to the taste."

Again, in preparing wine to keep it from fermenting, Columella says: "that your 'must' [that is, freshly extracted grape juice] may be always as sweet as it is new, thus proceed:

before you apply the press to the fruit, take the newest 'must' from the lake, put it into a new amphora, bung it up, and cover it very carefully with pitch, lest any water should enter; then immerse it in a cistern or pond of pure cold water, and allow no part of the amphora to remain above the surface. After forty days, take it out, and it will remain sweet for a year." The preservation of ancient wines as non-intoxicating is astounding and should put to rest forever the mistaken assumption many hold that all wine had to be intoxicating because the ancients could not keep it from fermenting. Columella further writes of a wine called *Amethyston* [meaning] "unintoxicating". He adds, that it was "a good wine", "harmless"; and called *iners* [weak] and would not affect the nerves.

Polybius, a Greek historian about a century before Jesus: "Among the Romans the women were forbidden to drink wine; they drank a wine which is called passum (Latine, Passum), and this was made from dried grapes or raisins. As a drink, it very much resembled 'Egosthenian' and 'Cretan', a sweet wine, and which is used for the purpose of allaying thirst."

Plutarch, a Greek historian and contemporary of the Apostles: "Wine is rendered old or feeble in strength when it is frequently filtered; this percolation makes it more pleasant to the palate; the strength of the wine is thus taken away, without any injury to its pleasing flavor. The strength being thus withdrawn or excluded, the wine neither inflames the head nor infests the mind and the passions, but is much more pleasant to drink. Doubtless defoecation takes away the spirit of potency that torments the head of the drinker; and this being removed, the wine is reduced to a state both mild, salubrious and wholesome" (Nott, 1857).

Works Cited

ACB. (2009, Mar 14). Retrieved Mar 14, 2009, from Associated Content/Business: *http://www.associatedcontent.com/article/200287/an_untapped_market_young_adults_that_pg2.html?cat=3*

ASA. (2009, Mar 13). Retrieved Mar 13, 2009, from Adolescent Substance Abuse: *http://www.adolescent-substance-abuse.com/binge-drinking-underage.html*

Augustine, S. (2000). Philip Schaff, The Nicene Fathers, electronic ed. (Garland, TX: Galaxie Software, 2000). Garland, TX.

Babor, T. (1986). *The Encyclopedia of Psychoactive Drugs* (Vol. 2). New York: Chelsea House Publishers.

Bacchiocchi, S. (2004). *Wine in the Bible: A Biblical Study of the Use of Alcoholic Beverages*. Berrien Springs: Biblical Perspectives.

Bank, J. C. (1892). *The British Controversialist & Literary Magazine*. London: Houlston and Wright.

Barnes, A. (2000). *Barnes Notes on the Bible, V. 12 John*. Rio, Wisconsin, USA.

Barnes, A. (n.d.). *Matthew 11*. Retrieved Mar 23, 2009, from *Barnes Notes on the New Testament*. *<http://www.studylight.org/com/bnn/view.cgi?book=mt&chapter=011>*.

Bespaloff, A. (1988). *The New Encyclopedia of Wine*. New York: William, Morrow and Company, Inc.

Bloom, A. (1987). *The Closing of the American Mind*. New York: Simon and Schuster.

Broadus, J. (1845, Summer). *Address to the Berryville Total Abstinence Society*. N/A.

Burleson, W. (2009). *Hardball Religion: Feeling the Fury of Fundamentalism*. Macon: Smyth & Helwys Publishing.

Cahn, S. M., & Haber, J. G. (1995). *20th Century Ethical Theory*. Prentice-Hall Inc.: Englewood Cliffs.

Califano, J. (1996). Fiction and Facts about Drug Legalization. *America, 174* (9), 7.

Cathcart, W. (Ed.). (1881). *The Baptist Encyclopedia* (Vol. III). Philadelphia: LOUIS H. EVERTS.

CDC. (2009, Mar 14). Retrieved Mar 14, 2009, from Centers for Disease Control and Prevention: *http://www.cdc.gov/alcohol/quickstats/binge_drinking.htm*

Chrysostom. (2000). Philip Schaff, The Nicene Fathers, electronic ed. Garland, TX.

Cooper, K. T. (1979). The Best Wine: John 2:1-11. *Westminster Theological Journal, 41* (2), 364-380.

Dagg, J. (1857). *Manual of Theology*. Harrisonburg: Gano Books.

Davis, J. J. (1985). *Evangelical Ethics: Issues Facing the Church Today*. Phillipsburg: Presbyterian and Reformed Publishing Company.

Devlin, K. (2009, Nov 11). *The Telegraph: UK*. Retrieved Mar. 3, 2009, from Teenage Girls Start Drinking at 13, New Study Shows: *http://www.telegraph.co.uk/news/3441619/EMBARGO-MID-NIGHT-Teenage-girls-drinking-from-a-younger-age-than-a-decade-ago.html*

Editorial. (1947, Feb 5). 'Moderation' and 'Profits'. *The Christian Century*, pp. 167-169.

Ellis, J. (1882). *The Wine Question in Light of the New Dispensation*. New York: N/A.

Encyclopedia of Alcohol. (2009, Mar 14). *Encyclopedia of Alcohol*. Retrieved Mar. 14, 2009, from enotes.com: *http://www.enotes.com/drugs-substances-encyclopedia/alco-hol/what-made?print=1*

Falk, A. (2008, Oct 2). *The Cornell Daily Sun*. Retrieved Mar. 3, 2009, from Administrators Against Lowering the Drinking Age: *http://cornellsun.com/node/32259*

Farrar, F. W. (1879). *Talks on Temperance*. N/A: National Temperance Society and Publication House.

Feinberg, J. S., & Feinberg, P. D. (1993). *Ethics for a Brave New World*. Wheaton: Crossway Books.

Field, L. C. (1883). *Oinos: The Bible Wine Question*. New York: Phillips & Hunt.

Fletcher, J. (1966). *Situation Ethics: The New Morality*. Philadelphia: The Westminster Press.

Francis J. Beckwith, Gregory Koukl. (1998). *Relativism: Feet Firmly Planted in Mid-Air*. Grand Rapids: Baker Books.

Geisler, N. (1989). *Christian Ethics: Options and Issues*. Grand Rapids: Baker Book House.

Geisler, N. L., & Feinberg, P. D. (1980). *Introduction to Philosophy: A Christian Perspective*. Grand Rapids: Baker Book House.

Gentry, J. K. (2001). *God Gave Wine: What the Bible Says About Alcohol*. Lincoln: Oakdown of MenschWerks.

Gordon, E. (1944). *Christ, The Apostles, and Wine*. Chicago: The Sunday School Times.

GW Magazine. (2009). Retrieved Feb 27, 2009, from *http://www.gwu.edu/~magazine/archive/2006_spring/docs/feature_civilwar.html*

Jeffers, A. (1975). Wine in the Bible: Weal or Woe? *The Western Commentator, 5* (Jul-Aug), 7.

King, A. R. (1947, Dec 17). The Ethics of Moderation. *The Christian Century*, pp. 1549-1551.

Knout, J. A. (1925). *The Origins of Prohibition* (Reissued, 1967 by Russell and Russell, A Division of Atheneum House, Inc. ed.). New York: Alfred A. Knoff, Inc.

Land, R., & Duke, B. (2008). The Christian and Alcohol. *Criswell Theological Review, 5* (2), 19-38.

Lee, D. E. (2009, February 25). *Assemblies of God, USA*. Retrieved February 21, 2009, from Assemblies of God, USA: *http://ag.org/top/Beliefs/Position_Papers/index.cfm*

Lees, F. R., Burns, D., & Lewis, T. (1870). *The Temperance Bible-Commentary: Giving at One View, Version, Criticism, and Exposition, in Regard to All Passages of Holy*

Writ Bearing on 'wine' and 'strong Drink', or Illustrating the Principles of the Temperance Reformation. New York: Sheldon & Co.

Lutzer, E. (1981). *The Necessity of Ethical Absolutes.* Grand Rapids: Zondervan Publishing House.

MacArthur, J. *The MacArthur Study Bible.*

Maguire, R. (1863). *The Miracles of Christ.* London: Weeks and Company.

Masters, P. (1992). *Should Christians Drink?: The Case for Total Abstinence.* London: The Wakeman Trust.

Morris, A. (2008, Dec 8). *New York Times Magazine.* Retrieved Mar 3, 2009, from Gender Bender: *http://nymag.com/news/features/52758/index1.html*

Morris, L. (1971). *The Gospel According to John.* Grand Rapids: Eerdmans Publishing Company.

Murray, J. (1957). *Principles of Conduct: Aspects of Biblical Ethics.* Grand Rapids: Eerdmans Publishing Company.

NEA. (2009). *National Education Association 2009 Handbook.* Washington, D.C.: National Education Association.

Norman Geisler, Frank Turek. (1998). *Legislating Morality: Is it wise? Is it Legal? Is it Possible?* Minneapolis: Bethany House Publishers.

Norman L. Geisler, Paul D. Feinberg. (1980). *Introduction to Philosophy: A Christian Perspective.* Grand Rapids: Baker Book House.

Nott, E. (1857). *Lectures on Temperance.* New York: Sheldon, Blakeman & Co.

Owen, J. J. (1860). *A Commentary, Critical, Expository, And Practical, On The Gospel Of John.* New York: Leavitt and Allen.

Owen, J. (1870). *Matthew.* Charles Scribner & Co.

Peele, S. (1989). *This Diseasing of America: Addiction Treatment Out of Control.* Lexington: Lexington Books.

Research, B. (2009). *EdStetzer.com.* Retrieved Mar 18, 2009, from EdStetzer.com:

http://blogs.lifeway.com/blog/edstetzer.com/2009/03/barna-how-many-have-a-biblical.html

Resolution. (1896). *Southern Baptist Convention.* Retrieved Feb. 21, 2009, from SBC.NET: http://www.sbc.net/resolutions/amResolution.asp?ID=46

Resolution, S. (1886). *Southern Baptist Convention.* Retrieved Feb 21, 2009, from SBC Net: *http://www.sbc.net/resolutions/amResolution.asp?ID=42*

Reynolds, S. M. (2003). *The Biblical Approach to Alcohol.* Glenside: Lorine L. Reynolds Foundation.

Richard Land, B. D. (2008, May 02). The Christian and Alcohol. *Criswell Theological Review*, 19-38.

Ritchie, W. (1866). *Scripture Testimony Against Intoxicating Wine.* N/A: Harvard University (Original); Republished by National Temperance Society and Publication House.

Rodney Stark, William Sims Bainbridge. (1997). *Religion, Deviance, and Social Control.* Routledge.

Rogers, J. C. (1979). The Dionysian Background of Ephesians 5:18. *Bibliotheca Sacra*, 250-257.

Samson, G. W. (1880). *The Divine Law As to Wines; Established by the Testimony of Sages, Physicians, and Legislators against the Use of Fermented and Intoxicating Wines; Confirmed by Their Provision of Unfermented Wines to Be Used for Medicinal and Sacramental Purposes.* New York: National Temperance Society and Publication House.

Schaeffer, F. (1982). *The Complete Works of Francis Schaeffer: A Christian Worldview.* Westchester, IL, USA: Crossway Books.

Schenectady County, New York History and Genealogy. (1938). Retrieved Feb 26, 2009, from SCHENECTADY DIGITAL HISTORY ARCHIVE: *http://www.schenectadyhistory.org/people/ohof/nott.html*

Smith, A. J. (1946, Aug 7). Where 'Temperance' Fails, *The*

Christian Century, pp. 961-962.

Stein, R. H. (1975, June 20). Wine-Drinking in New Testament Times. *Christianity Today*, 9-11.

Stuart, M. (1848). *Scriptural View of the Wine-Question*. New York: Levitt, Trow and Company, Printers.

Tait, J. W. (N/D). When The People Take Poison No More: "Alcohol, Science, and Common-Sense Realism in the Methodist Eucharistic Grape Juice Debate, 1830-1900". *Weselyn Theological Society*.

Teachout, R. P. (1979). The Use of "Wine" in the Old Testament. *Unpublished Dissertation Presented to the Faculty of Semitics and Old Testament Studies, Dallas Theological Seminary*, 462. Dallas, TX.

Tenney, M. (1981). *The Gospel of John* (Vol. 9). Grand Rapids, Michigan: The Zondervan Corporation.

Timberlake, J. H. (1963). *Prohibition and the Progressive Movement: 1900-1920*. Atheneum: Harvard University Press.

Trench, R. (1850). *Notes on the Miracles of Our Lord*. New York: D. Appleton & Company.

Trimmer, J. M. (1946, Aug 28). The Menace of Moderation. *The Christian Century*, pp. 1037-1038.

Warfield, B. B. (2003). *Revelation and Inspiration* (Vol. I). Dallas: Digital Publications.

Wechsler, H. (2008, Dec 8). *Insufficient Evidence for Lowering the Drinking Age*. Retrieved Mar. 3, 2009, from The Harvard Crimson: *http://www.thecrimson.com/article.aspx?ref=525812*

Wickersham, et al. (1931, Jan 7). *The Wickersham Commission Report on Alcohol Prohibition*. Retrieved Feb 26, 2009, from Report on the Enforcement of the Prohibition Laws of the United States: *http://www.drugtext.org/library/reports/wick/Default.htm*

Williamson, G. I. (1999). *Wine in the Bible and the Church*. G. I. Williamson.